ALL WHO WILL LISTEN

Claire Patterson

LifeRich Publishing books may be ordered through booksellers or by contacting:

LifeRich Publishing
1663 Liberty Drive
Bloomington, IN 47403
www.liferichpublishing.com
844-686-9607

Cover and interior art by Pat Bethell

ISBN: 978-1-4897-4942-0 (sc)
ISBN: 978-1-4897-4943-7 (hc)
ISBN: 978-1-4897-4941-3 (e)

Library of Congress Control Number: 2023918416

Print information available on the last page.

LifeRich Publishing rev. date: 10/11/2023

"Someone special gifted me with Claire's first two books. As a convert, *Through Mary's Eyes,* helped me begin my relationship with Mary. I could feel how deeply Our Blessed Mother loved her Son and his followers.

"Claire's second book, *Finding Grace Through Mary's Eyes,* impressed me with her courage and openness in revealing her private life with husband Duke and the spiritual warfare that devotion to Mary provokes from the Enemy.

"In Claire's third book, she invites people to share their own stories of intercessions by God, Mary and the angels. In a digital world, where many forces compete for our attention, *All Who Will Listen* reminds us that God is with us daily, blessing and protecting; our challenge is learning to listen."

William Lewis Klein, author of *Sign For Our Time: God's Salvation Plan and the Symbolism of Snow*

"Claire is an 'Energy Bunny' for the Lord, as she has moved with the Holy Spirit on every possibility she could fulfill for her God and our Blessed Mother.

"In addition to her credits already listed, she is a faithful member of our Eucharistic Prayer Group as we meet weekly to pray the Patriotic Rosary. Her past career as a school administrator, and love of children, took her to our Diocesan Catholic Children's Home where she volunteered and mentored those children with her love, heart and soul.

"God bless you, Claire. He continues to watch where you follow Him!"

Pat Bethell

"I first met Claire when I attended a monthly speaker session at my parish. She provided beautiful slides of her trips and shared how her husband saw and talked to our Mother Mary. I was so intrigued that I couldn't wait to buy her book. Since I was a little girl, I've wanted to grow my relationship with Mary. God spoiled me when I read Claire's first book, *Through Mary's Eyes*. As I read, I could feel many of Mary's emotions, especially her DEEP love for her Son and His apostles.

"Claire's second book again touched my heart. I learned from the time of my First Communion that the devil enjoys pulling us away from our Lord whenever he gets the chance. *Finding Grace through Mary's Eyes* made me more aware of the devil's relentless efforts. I've had the joy of working with Claire since our Lord asked her to do her third book. I'm a story lover, so naturally I LOVE her third book. If you are like me, you are going to enjoy these stories. All of Claire's books have touched my heart and helped me grow closer to Mary and Her Awesome Son. Thank you so very much, Claire!"

Pam Ryan-Rettig

"God always has a plan. As you read this book with an open mind and an open heart, you will see how He uses angels and humans to be a part of His plan. Will you listen for, and answer His call?"

Joe Gering

"Claire Patterson's books are well written, faith affirming and provide hope. They are easy reads and give perspective on Mary's life and God's power."

Robert (Bob) Flaherty, Jr.

Dedication

This book is dedicated to our good and holy priests. They have forsaken the world so they can lead us on pilgrimages, inspire us during retreats, baptize, confirm, marry, anoint and bury us. They cleanse our souls through the sacrament of confession and bring Jesus Christ to us through the Holy Eucharist.

I also want to dedicate this book to our deacons, consecrated Sisters and Brothers who have served us well and taught us so much throughout our lives.

I also dedicate this book to my dear brother-in-Law, Pastor Ron Patterson. Ron, and men like him, turn their back on the world's materialism and wickedness. They dedicate their lives to teach and bring others to the mercy of God.

By their inspiring lives, they all lead us to our eternal reward.

"To shine on those who sit in darkness and death's shadow,
to guide our feet onto the path of peace." Luke 1:79

In conformity with the decrees by Pope Urban VIII, the author and contributors recognize and accept that the final authority regarding the messages and testimonies presented herein, rests with the Holy See of Rome, to whose judgement they willingly submit.

Upon the approval of Pope Paul VI, on October 14, 1966, with the abolition of previous Canons 1399 and 2318 of the former Canonical Code, and the decree of the Congregation for the Propagation of the Faith, S.A.S. 58 1186, publications about new appearances, revelations, prophecies, miracles, etc. have been allowed to be distributed and read by the faithful without the express permission of the Church, providing they contain nothing which contravenes faith and morals. This means that no imprimatur is necessary when distributing information on new apparitions not yet judged or approved by the Church.

The editors and publisher have no evidence of the validity of any of the stories related in this book; however, they have no reason to believe that they are not genuine as offered by the individual writers. We leave it to the reader to discern the truth.

The messages in Chapter 12 have been validated by a committee of Marian scholars and devotees, consisting of Fr. Leroy Smith, Fr. Lawrence Sweeney, Fr. Donald Rinfret, and Jerry Ross, who is the author of several books regarding Our Lady of Light[19]. After three months of interviews and examination of the messages given to Calvin (Duke) Patterson between July 2001 and August 2003, the committee stated, in the Our Lady of the Holy Spirit Center[18] Newsletter of August/September 2003, **"Calvin Patterson and his messages have been affirmed authentic and worthy of instruction."**

Bible References included in this book have been taken from the 1992 publication of St. Joseph's Edition of the New American Bible, Catholic Book Publishing Co. New York, unless otherwise noted.

Cover and interior art by Pat Bethell.

About the Cover

Each of us, unless we are a hermit living in a cave, have lives cluttered with distractions that create a cacophony of sound which drowns out God's "still small voice." We need to find ways to reduce and remove these unnecessary distractions, at least for a part of each day, so we can focus on God.

Carve out some special time to turn to Him, love Him, praise Him, worship Him, and thank Him.

As often as possible, shut the door on distractions and give God our full attention. Let us all learn to be more aware of His voice and listen to Him.

"Be still and confess that I am God! I am exalted among the nations, exalted on the earth." Psalm 46:11

Acknowledgements

I want to extend a tremendous "THANK YOU" to those serving on my team.

Without their talents, dedication and many hours of editing, researching, and promoting, this book would never have been available to you, the reader.

They are my faithful friends and colleagues: Pat Bethell, Mary Ann Brausch, Susie Curtis, Terri Lachtrupp, Pam Rettig, Kathy Thamann and Marianne Tomlinson.

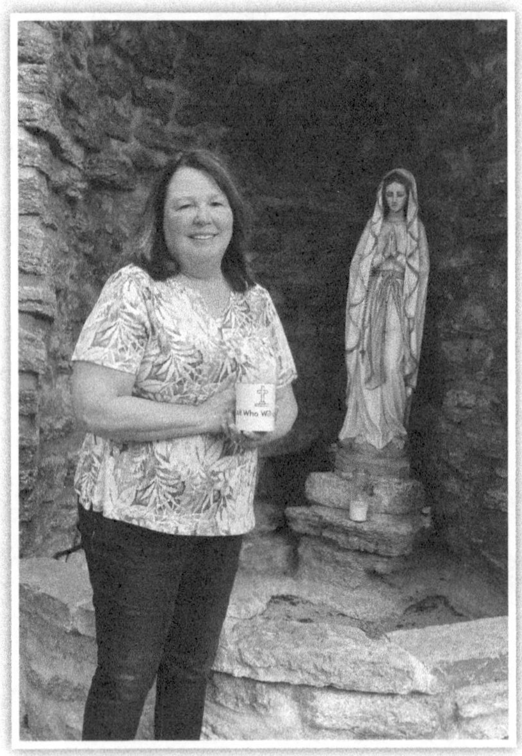

Also, I wish to thank the many authors who have generously donated their stories of hope, struggle, faith, and trust in God. Without their contributions this would be a very thin and meaningless book.

Many thanks to Michael Brocker for technical assistance.

And I give all glory to God, who inspired us to take on this task. Without Him, we are nothing.

"I am the vine; you are the branches. Whoever remains in Me and I in him will bear much fruit, because without Me, you can do nothing." John 15:5.

Foreword

This FOREWORD recalls extraordinary experiences in the life of Duke (Calvin) Patterson, husband of Claire, the author of this book. As a long-time friend, I was privileged to witness some of the events as they unfolded.

My husband and I met Duke and Claire Patterson when we were participating in a Catholic Marriage Encounter program together in the early 1990's.

Couples in our "Circle" took turns hosting monthly meetings in their homes. Praying, discussing sacramental marriage, and sharing joys and hardships were techniques utilized to strengthen each marriage and build friendships.

Claire and Duke appeared in many ways quite different from each other. Claire seemed poised, engaging, self-assured and a devout Catholic; Duke was quiet by nature, nervous in a crowd, and took frequent trips outside to smoke. He was a former Seventh Day Adventist, who alluded to having had a difficult childhood. Duke loved to garden "…in straight lines and right angles only." Both had no air of pretense whatsoever; they were likable from the start.

The fact that we met at each other's homes was a very bonding experience. We were together in our Circle for a few years, but sadly, we eventually lost touch with each other.

About ten years later I read in the newsletter of Our Lady of the Holy Spirit Center[18] that a man named Duke (Calvin) Patterson – there could only be one of them! – was receiving messages from the Blessed Mother and other saints; at times, even from Jesus! Mary instructed Duke to: "Tell All Who Will Listen."

When I read that, I laughed with joy for three days – there was no way on earth that Duke Patterson could be misguided, faking it or seeking attention. I rejoiced knowing that heaven was indeed touching earth in a downright miraculous way.

The fruits of these messages led Claire and Duke to fast on bread and water Wednesdays and Fridays. They attended daily Mass together, read the Bible, and prayed all fifteen decades of the Rosary. Talks were given to small groups, sharing the messages Duke had received, as the Blessed Mother had requested. They were also inspired to start a weekly prayer group at Our Lady of the Holy Spirit Center, regularly attended by roughly a dozen people. I was privileged to be a part of that group.

We would pray the Joyful, Sorrowful and Glorious Mysteries at first, then added the Luminous Mysteries in 2002, when they were introduced by Pope St. John Paul ll.[26]

Duke did not just concentrate on each Biblical Mystery during the rosary; at times, he was blessed to be transported into the scene, experiencing the Mystery as if he were actually there. Despite medical difficulties, including several knee replacement surgeries, he would kneel on the carpet in the Center's library during the Sorrowful Mysteries with tears streaming down his face. He was shaken watching Jesus being battered and crucified.

"Ours were the sufferings He bore, ours the sorrows
He carried... by His Stripes we are healed..."
Isaiah 53:4-5

One day I asked Duke if he would have lunch with me so I could ask him questions about his experiences. It was during that meal that I saw in him a sensitive, compassionate, loving heart of gold and I knew, then, why heaven had chosen him for this mission:

"... to confound the wisdom of this world." 1 Corinthians: 1:27

Satan would at times appear to Duke and call him "a maggot."

On a Thursday evening, before the Rosary group started, Duke said the Blessed Mother had a message for me, personally. Please understand that messages from Our Lady are timeless; and although this one was specifically directed to me, it could also apply to almost anyone. When you read this, see if it applies to you, as well.

"It causes me to cry tears of joy whenever just one of my children makes the decision to join me in Glorifying my Son. If you want someone to pray with you, I am only a prayer away. What mother would not come when her child calls out to her? What is of utmost importance is not the love I (Blessed Mother) feel in my heart, but rather the love you feel in yours."
Message given on November 20, 2008.

The way I see it:

Sincere prayer, a surrendering of the heart to our true and living God, helps thin the veil that separates heaven and earth. (See Isaiah 25:6-8) It seems the veil was lifted for Duke Patterson with messages and glimpses of the lives of Jesus and Mary, to be shared with all who will listen. He was given messages about becoming holy and giving God the love He alone is due.

What I learned from Duke:

1. God the Father, Son and Holy Spirit, Mary, angels and saints are very real and much closer to us than we think.
2. Prayer is like breathing - it is a necessity.
3. God's Love for each of us is personal and awesome beyond words.
4. Daily Rosary, recited with faith and love, is a true weapon against the enemy of our souls.

In this, Claire Patterson's third book, ordinary people share their experiences of those moments when the veil between heaven and earth was briefly thinned for them. It is hoped that upon reading this, your faith will be strengthened and you will know, without a doubt, that you are loved and cherished by God.

To God be All Glory,
Marianne Tomlinson

Introduction

"The Lord was not in the wind...The Lord was not in the earthquake...The Lord was not in the fire...there was a tiny whispering sound..." 1 Kings 19:11-13

I have written and talked about the many miraculous events that my husband, Duke, experienced during and after our trip to Medjugorje in 2001. Because his spiritual incidents far out-shadowed mine, I have seldom mentioned what I was sensing and witnessing.

Since many people have encouraged me to share my memories, I am divulging several amazing incidents herein.

I have also included stories from over thirty contributing authors about their sometimes life-changing experiences. These writers are normal people; those you meet in the grocery store, those who cut your hair, those who teach your children, and those who love to do crafts. However, through God's grace, they have received guidance, cures, and answered prayers. Some of these stories reflect current world events, such as COVID; others are memories from the author's youth, and everything in between.

"This is why I speak to them in parables, because they look but do not see and hear but do not listen...." Matthew 13:13

We must never think that we cannot have such experiences ourselves. We are all God's children, equal in his eyes. If you don't feel His love, know that He is always with you. Miracles happen every day. We just need to open our minds and hearts to recognize them.

God often answers our prayers and directs our lives with what has been called a "still small voice."

"Listen to Him." Mark 9:17

Sometimes I hear that voice at unexpected times. I don't hear it in my ears; I hear it in my heart. I am urged to do something I would not normally do, and it is often outside my comfort zone. I am not a courageous person by nature, so reaching out to a stranger can feel awkward. When I try to ignore it, the voice can be persistent. I have never regretted following that voice from heaven, even though it has often meant stepping into unfamiliar territory.

Throughout the years, I have been given messages in my heart when I am praying intently. Sometimes the insight is as simple as: "Pick up the phone and call Kathy." Sometimes the nudge tells me to give someone money or assistance. More often than not, my subsequent action, in response to God's bidding, has been the exact gift the person needed at the time.

I always try to consider where the voice or impulse is coming from. One must discern if it is a holy voice, or an evil voice.

"Beloved, do not imitate evil, but imitate good. Whoever does what is good is of God; whoever does what is evil has never seen God." 3 John 1:11

What is important is that I endeavor to do what I am being asked to do, when I have sensed that the voice is from heaven. Then it is up to me to overcome my feelings of laziness, shyness, or fear.

"Lean on, trust in, and be confident in the Lord with all your heart and mind and do not rely on your own insight or understanding. In all your ways know, recognize, and acknowledge Him, and He will direct and make straight and plain your paths." Proverbs 3:5-6

So, it all boils down to a few things. Keep your heart pure, so that you can be receptive to the urgings of God, and be better able to judge *if it is* from God. Find some quiet time each day, so that you can hear His voice. Put on your spiritual armor daily. Be brave, selfless, wise, strong, and humble, so that when you hear that still small voice you can unreservedly follow God's will. This is not an easy task, but as Jesus said,

"Be perfect, therefore, as your Heavenly Father is perfect."
Matthew 5:48

We need to at least try, don't we?

I pray that you will reap benefits from the stories herein. They are not all about listening to the voice; some are about angels, sent from God, to help and protect us. Some are about the power of prayer, or about overcoming adversity. These are all signs from God that He is near, and that He loves us more than we can ever comprehend.

I am very grateful for the generosity and dedication of the contributing authors. They are freely offering their testimonies to you. It is my prayer that these stories touch your heart, as much as they have touched mine.

"...You say I am a king. For this I was born and for this I came into the world, to testify to the truth. Everyone who belongs to the truth listens to my voice." John 18:37

Claire A. Patterson

Contents

*"….This is My beloved Son, with whom I am well pleased; **listen** to Him."*
Matthew 17: 5

Part I – That Still Small Voice

Part III – Touched by Heaven

PART I

That Still Small Voice

CHAPTER 1

A Persistent Voice

"...Speak Lord, your servant is listening..." 1 Samuel 3:9

"Check on Dorothy"

Sue P.

On March 14, 2017, my neighbor, Dorothy, was ninety-two years old. I knew her from my church. She was sweeping her steps that morning when she fell onto her steep gravel driveway. She could not move. Dorothy began praying for someone to come and help her. She was conscious, lying in pain with a broken hip, for many hours. The weather that day was blustery cold with intermittent sleet and snow.

That same morning, I arose and as usual, had my morning devotions and prayers.

I had several appointments that morning, so I left home around 9:00 a.m. and returned around 1:00 p.m.

Then I got busy working on crafts for my daughter's wedding. Around 4:00 p.m. I heard a voice, clear as a bell, in my head saying, "Check on Dorothy." I called her immediately, but there was no answer.

I looked up the road and saw that her car was in the driveway. I assumed Dorothy was just resting and I thought, "She must be napping.

I'll just call her later." Besides, it was so cold and nasty outside and I didn't really want to get all bundled up to run up the long hill to her house. Waiting to call her also gave me more time to complete my crafts. I didn't realize the urgency of the internal voice and I was totally distracted with my projects.

Then, around 7:00 p.m. the voice came clearly again, "Go check on Dorothy, now!" My stomach sank! I felt sick as I realized that Dorothy may be in some danger and I had let so many hours go by.

I called her again and there was no answer. Instantly I knew something must be terribly wrong. So, I got all bundled up to endure the weather and ran up to her house. As I got closer to her house, I saw her lying in her gravel driveway. Her head was facing down the hill, and she was covered in snow and frozen stiff.

I immediately called 911. Then I got a pillow for her head and several blankets to cover her up as we waited for the ambulance to arrive. Parts of her body were purple, so the EMTs put her under heat lamps and a blanket warmer to raise her body temperature back to normal. I prayed she wouldn't get sick. Praise the Lord, she didn't.

The paramedics told me if I had gotten there any later, Dorothy would have frozen to death.

The two lessons that I learned from this experience are:

1. We can sometimes get so busy that we don't listen to God's voice speaking to us. But when we slow down, we have a better chance of hearing His voice.
2. We always need to obey the voice of God. I heard a plain and clear voice, yet I pushed it aside, because I was busy doing my own thing! As I look back on it now, I ask myself, "What was I thinking? Why would His Spirit speak to me so clearly if Dorothy was only sleeping?" I should have obeyed that voice immediately! It was not a scream or shout; yet it was a loud, firm urgent voice. God was trying hard to get my attention! Yet, I was too busy to obey it. As a result of my negligence, my neighbor had lain on the cold hard gravel drive from 10:00 a.m. until 7:00 p.m., helplessly enduring harsh exposure to snow and sleet!

Now I listen and obey immediately when I hear that voice! God blessed Dorothy's faithfulness by answering her prayer, and used me to save her life because He cares for His children! I praise the Lord God for using me, and allowing me to be a part of His plan to help my neighbor survive.

"Fear not, I am with you; be not dismayed; I am your God. I will strengthen you, and help you, and uphold you with My right hand of justice."
Isaiah 41:10

Listening to that Still Small Voice Can Save a Life

Kiersten Baughman

One day my mother was telling me about a strange phone conversation that my Grandmother had the day before with a friend of hers, whom we'll call "Dee." Some of the details sent chills up my spine. "It was almost as if she had someone else in the room with her," my mother said. This triggered the first God incident, where I felt the urge to further investigate what was really going on with Dee. Dee always ended statements by calling people "honey," and on this occasion, my grandmother said, she had not. This also struck me as another red flag, but I didn't quite know why.

I suddenly sensed a need to have someone check on Dee face-to-face to make sure she was okay. As her home was not far from where I was living, I suggested to my mom that we drop in to visit her. My mom was busy with tasks and found this a bit of an annoyance, but agreed that we could drive by the next day.

When we arrived, I had a chilling feeling, but still expected Dee to answer her door and quell the fear I was experiencing. We knocked and knocked, called her name, and called her phone, but no one ever answered or came to the door.

The thought occurred to me that Dee could have been forcibly removed from her home. Another God incident came the next day, which was that I knew we couldn't stop until we located Dee and ensured that she was safe. At this point, my mom was a bit more concerned than she had been three days before, but she still was not convinced, like I was, that something was wrong.

Neither my mom nor I knew much about Dee, but mom was aware that Dee watched a few children during the week, and mom knew how to reach the family of the children. I reasoned that they would probably know her pretty well, since they relied on her for childcare. I remember talking to this person on the phone explaining that I didn't really know what was going on, and was hoping everything was fine, but that we just really needed to talk to Dee to make sure she was okay. To my pleasant surprise, this woman thanked me for the call and said she didn't know anything but would try to reach Dee.

God still tugged on my heart, giving me an idea that there might be one other way to reach Dee – through her children. Mom was pretty sure one of her sons was an electrician, so I researched names and businesses in the local community. By God's Grace, I reached the right person a day later, but he had not heard from his mother either.

By the time her son went to check on her, Dee had been in her home for several days. He had to let himself in with his spare key. As it turns out, Dee had suffered from a massive life-changing stroke just before my grandmother had called, and that is why she was acting so strangely on the phone. That's also why she was not calling her "honey" in her usual way.

Had it not been for my persistence in following the continuous urges I felt, despite very little personal connection to Dee, her fate would likely have been much different.

As I write this, Dee has made a full recovery, and is back to saying, "Honey," to her friends. I will forever be glad that I listened to "that still small voice" and I encourage you to do so also. You just might save someone's life!

"Jesus, I am Learning to Love You."

Anonymous

Back in 1981 my sister, Ann, made a Cursillo[5] weekend in Atlanta. She was so excited about it, that when she came to visit us, she told us all about how it had changed her life. Both my husband, Farrell, and I decided we would make a weekend as well. My sister volunteered to be Farrell's sponsor for his entrance into the Cursillo Community. He had a very positive experience, and I could hardly wait for the next women's weekend.

When the January weekend came closer, I asked my principal for a Friday off from teaching. She granted my request.

I had been told that there would be a series of talks, and after each one, we would get to discuss what we learned. Of course, there were extra activities like Holy Mass each day and opportunities for confession.

On Saturday at 11:00 a.m., right before Mass, we were told by the weekend leader, "This time when you go to Holy Communion, don't talk to God about your laundry list of what you want. This time, just tell God you love Him." I thought, "OK! I can do that!"

When it was time for Holy Communion, I walked up and received our Lord. Then as I walked back to my pew, that thought came back to my mind; to tell God I love Him. After I folded my hands I said, "Jesus, I ask for You to bless my family and the children at school." Then, because of all I had heard during the Cursillo experiences I said, "Jesus, I'm learning to love you." And right away, a change came over me. I heard an audible voice say to me: "**Joan, I love you too.**" I looked up, and saw that everyone in the room had their heads down praying. It was then I knew: God had spoken **just** to me!

After mass I rushed up to the weekend leader and told her what had happened. She said, "Oh Joan! That is wonderful! I am so happy for you!" So was I! But I had no idea what it meant for me, or what God had in mind for me.

I drove to my job on the following Monday morning, but somehow my world was different. My second graders had not changed. The other teachers had not changed, and my principal was the same as when I had left; but something had changed in my life.

As a second-grade teacher, I had days that were better than others. What I mean is, sometimes the children loved to talk, and when they were talking and would not listen, my ability to teach would go down the drain. So, I decided to ask Jesus to help me in my classroom.

I purchased a spiral notebook and used it to write down things that happened at school. As I wrote, I asked Jesus what I should do. I was also thinking, "How can I get control of my classroom?"

Guess what? Jesus had a plan! He placed his thoughts in my head as I journaled each evening. His plan involved getting me to trust Him. Usually, I raised my voice to get the students' attention, and when the children heard me over their talking, they stopped and listened. But that method involved raising my stress level.

So, I asked Jesus to help. This is what He said to me: "Explain your relationship with Me to the children. Tell them how you love Me. Tell them I want them to learn all the lessons in the second grade. They cannot do that if they do not listen to you."

Jesus told me, "When you begin to talk and the students are not listening, say this to the children, 'I want you to be quiet. I will not say anything else.'" Jesus then told me to wait and watch. He told me to close my eyes and pray to God for His help.

So, I said and did just what Jesus had told me to do. Guess what happened? The children started getting quiet. And right at that moment, one of them said, "She's praying!" Then it really got quiet. At that moment, I opened my eyes and thanked them and began to teach again.

And, no, they didn't continue to stay quiet every day for the rest of the year! I needed to ask Jesus for help again and again. But His instructions and my action worked each time. I tried to help other teachers use that plan, but they must have given up on it. Maybe they needed to make a Cursillo weekend! Or maybe God wanted them to get to know Him better.

Now that was the first part of God's plan for me. Here comes the next part:

Because I taught the second grade, every year we prepared the students to receive two very important Sacraments. The first was Reconciliation (Confession), and the second was First Holy Communion.

When our new principal came to our school, a group of teachers said that there were many things we were currently doing with which she did not agree. It became a stressful situation. She started chiding me for everything she thought I was doing wrong. She did not communicate to me that I was an incompetent teacher, but, without fail, every time something went wrong in the hallway, on the playground, or lunchroom, she was always right there to witness it. I cannot tell you how many times I went to Reconciliation while she was our principal!

It was right in the middle of these difficulties that I took a day off of school to make my Cursillo weekend.

I'll bet you are wondering how in the world this situation could be resolved. You are correct, if you think it involved a certain relationship with Jesus.

On the morning the second graders received their First Holy Communion, I received another message from Jesus. This one was not an audible message; it was a thought. Jesus spoke to my heart and said, "I want you to apologize to the principal." I said to Him, "I <u>will</u> apologize, but please, give me the words." Then the message, "**I will**," came to my mind.

That morning the teachers walked the students over to church from our classrooms. The students walked up the center aisle preceding the altar servers and the priest. We teachers sat in the back with our principal.

The other second grade teachers begged me to sit next to the principal. I thought, "OK God, I will need those words now!" Well, right before the handshake of peace, the words came to me. She turned to me, and I whispered into her ear, "I'm so sorry I hurt you." She answered, "Oh you are such a wonderful girl!"

Soon after that, I walked up to the altar to assist as a Eucharistic Minister[7]. While I was standing there, a beautiful feeling came over me. It was like all the angels descended over the altar to be there with Jesus. I could sense that they were there. It was so beautiful, but my eyes could not see it; just my soul.

Oh God, I do not deserve your help! But I thank you! And I am learning to love you more and more!

Spiritual Motherhood of Priests

Anonymous

In 2012, I was working for three doctors as a transcriptionist. I did this at home and everything was automated; I could have carried on a conversation while I typed.

One day I received an email from a distant friend of mine. She sent a flier to me about a program called "Spiritual Motherhood of Priests" from the Archdiocese of Cincinnati, because she knew I had two sons in the seminary.

They were offering a one-day seminar in Cincinnati. I lived in Kentucky, just across the Ohio River, in a completely different diocese. After looking over the flier, I decided not to attend, so, I put it aside.

However, the idea of the program stayed heavily on my mind. The Holy Spirit was relentless. I kept thinking about it, telling myself that I cannot go to that program. I felt this pounding on my head constantly. It was the Holy Spirit again. I kept thinking about that seminar. I finally realized that it was the will of God that I should go, even though I kept telling myself, "I'm not from that diocese!"

About two days before the seminar was to take place, I called the number on the flier. I asked the woman on the phone if someone from outside of the Diocese of Cincinnati could attend. She said that there would be a lot of women from all over the United States coming to the seminar. "You should come."

I got there early, just to get a sense of what they might be doing. I was given many handouts, so I sat down in the front pews of the church to read them. I learned about the "Heart" of the "Spiritual Motherhood of Priests" program in a booklet entitled, "Eucharistic Adoration[1] for the Sanctification of Priests and Spiritual Maternity."

The Archbishop concelebrated the Holy Mass with many other priests. After Mass there were talks by the Archbishop, rectors of the seminarians, seminarians, mothers of priests, and other priests. One woman told us about the program in her parish. She passed out packets following her talk but they ran out when she got to me. This was actually a blessing of the Holy Spirit. She said hurriedly, "Just google it." As soon as I got home, I did as she suggested.

Much to my surprise, I saw that this program was not just in Cincinnati, Ohio, but all over the world. Women were praying for priests with Eucharistic Adoration in many countries! So, I started calling women across the United States.

The programs were working differently in each diocese, according to how the women in that area were permitted to operate with their Bishop's permission and guidance. The commonality was that they all had Eucharistic Adoration as their foundation!

One leader explained the program very well. "Eucharistic Adoration is the central focus of each Spiritual Motherhood program throughout the world. It can be operated according to how the women in each area are permitted to do things, but Eucharistic Adoration is a MUST!"

After talking to ten women in ten different states, I had an idea what I would do. I still did transcription at home, but I was thinking all the time about the Spiritual Motherhood Program.

The Holy Spirit continued to pester me to get something started in our diocese.

Since the heart of this program is Eucharistic Adoration, I went to Adoration for reflection and guidance. I even borrowed an hour from the woman who came in after me. Then I spent a lot of time putting our program together. The Holy Spirit gave me a lot of help. After many weeks, I had a plan.

Now what? I didn't know what to do with my plan. It seemed that the Holy Spirit was urging me to call someone. "Who should I call?", I yelled out in between my transcription sentences. I opened the phone book (yes, a phone book) and looked over the Diocese of Covington's phone numbers. I said, "Holy Spirit, who should I call????"

I was led to call the Vocation Director and made an appointment. He was excited to meet me! I was surprised! Did the Holy Spirit get to him too?

When I got to his office, he was ready for me. Father had many papers already spread across his nice clean desk. They were the <u>same</u> papers I had brought for him. How did this happen? It turns out that this "Spiritual Motherhood of Priests" program had already been initiated three times in our Diocese but had failed to continue. This priest was hoping that I was the one person who could make it happen.

Did Father already know that the Holy Spirit was pushing me? I felt that I had to work fast, but I needed the Bishop's approval. The Vocation Director said he would get the approval for me. I waited a month and he didn't call me. I finally called him. He apologized saying that he had been assigned two parishes to take care of and did not have time anymore to help me with my project.

He sent me to the Vicar General. When I finally connected with him, I talked quickly with the ten minutes he had given me to explain what I wanted. He said that he would call me back in a week. I called him after two weeks. I was as relentless as the Holy Spirit! I was learning from the best.

I never did have a meeting with the Vicar General. He finally just told me over the phone to get started with my "little prayer group" and get back with him after the first of the year. I started right away, but I didn't have a "little prayer group". So, I told all my friends, who told all their friends, who told more friends.

We had our first induction ceremony with forty-five women; most of whom I didn't even know. It was wonderful! The Holy Spirit taught me about how to do things on the computer, make prayer cards, programs, and even a spread sheet to keep a record of the priests who were adopted and the Spiritual Mothers' names. I was busy with the Holy Spirit on my shoulder.

As I write this, we have over three hundred women in our program. There is even a priest who helps me get appointments with pastors to recruit more women. We recently had the Bishop concelebrate a Mass for our Spiritual Mothers with a reception celebrating our ten-year anniversary. The Holy Spirit put that together as well! I just helped Him. He is running this program! I just follow. It works better that way!

CHAPTER 2

A Nudge to Go in Another Direction

"Many are the plans in a man's heart, but it is the decision of the Lord that endures."
Proverbs 19:21

"Check in the Restroom"

Claire Patterson

In 1995 I was the Assistant Principal for a career-technical school. It was my job to deal with the disciplinary issues, after the high-school teachers had tried their best with other methods.

One day I was making my rounds through the building when I got an idea to walk into the Adult Education nurses' restroom. I had never walked into that room before; my job was working with the high school students - not the adults. It was an illogical place for me to investigate, but the Holy Spirit urged me to enter.

I found one of our high school students on the floor in distress. She was considering suicide because she had recently found out she was pregnant. Her father was a minister and her parents were very strict. The student said that her mom and dad were so infuriated with her that they threatened to disown her because of the shame she was bringing to the family.

I was able to comfort her at that moment, and then refer her to someone who could work with her parents and provide support for the pregnancy.

Fortunately, the option of abortion was never considered, and the parents were persuaded to accept their daughter back into the family with love.

The Goodness of God

Colleen Read

It was 4:00 a.m. and I was wide awake. I began to think about a troubling situation involving a group of friends. I had been angry about what had happened recently and was composing an email in my head that I intended to send out to these friends. The fault did not lie totally with them, as I had not expressed my feelings before. Nonetheless, I allowed myself to feel justified with the resentment I was experiencing. I knew I would try to control my anger and frustration, but I also knew that some of those feelings would leak through my email message. Once I finally got up for the day, around 9:30 a.m., I did my prayer and reflection time. One of the reflections I read really hit me. I looked up and said, "OK God, these words were meant for me! I got it!"

One story was about a woman who was justifiably angry, but she used her anger to run another five miles on the treadmill. (My reaction to anger is usually to eat chocolate and say, "So there!"). I felt that in my situation, my anger was also justified but my reaction was going to be more of a "poor me" response as I composed the email. So, I decided <u>not</u> to send that email after all.

I love it when the Holy Spirit sends us whispers when we need them. We do not often get shouts or peels of thunder.

I had lunch that same day with a couple of friends and then after lunch I ran into a cousin at Kroger's. I witnessed to all three of those women about my Holy Spirit moment that morning. This is discipleship. This is what we are called to do. We cannot keep God's moments to ourselves.

I had another experience like this last year. I had asked God for an answer regarding what I should do about returning to my job at a local hospital. I was again in prayer one morning, when it dawned on me that He had answered me the night before. I just did not realize it at the time.

I had gathered with a group of women from church the evening before. One person asked if I would drive Kate home as I would be heading in that direction. After I dropped off my passenger, I decided to cut through the hospital campus to bring an item to my brother. I glanced at the main entrance of the hospital as I passed by. A very strong feeling hit me that made me realize I just could not walk through those doors again.

You see, the trauma and stress I had experienced as a greeter there during the COVID pandemic came flooding back to me. During those dark days, visitors to the hospital not only complained about the restrictions, they also yelled at me, lied to me, and sometimes swore at me on a daily basis. I had come to dread my job of welcoming visitors.

It did not dawn on me at that time, but God had orchestrated the ride I was asked to give to Kate. It was not until my reflection the next morning that I realized I had received the answer I had prayed about. I believe that, had I not experienced the terrible flashbacks while on the hospital grounds, I would possibly have returned to work there. But my panic generated by the trip through the hospital campus helped me to realize that I was not yet ready to return to my former job.

I used to write reflections in the early 2000's, mostly for a group at church. I'm always amazed at how some simple words affect people. The same occurred with this most recent reflection. I pretty much saw it as no big deal! But that was not how this was perceived by some of my friends, and I am thankful to the Holy Spirit for that. It is sort of like when you visit a garage sale. Some small little trinket can be exactly what another person is looking for.

These things happen all the time, but I have learned that I need to see them for what they are. We often feel that God is not listening or not answering us. But he does answer, all the time. We just need to open our eyes and ears.

Bargaining with God

Claire Patterson

The year was 2003. It was a very hot day with the temperature above ninety degrees. I was in a hurry to get to the pharmacy to have a prescription filled for my husband, who had just been released from the hospital. I was driving up a steep hill when I passed an elderly lady walking down the hill on the other side of the street. The voice in my heart said, "Pick her up."

I tried to argue with the voice. "Can I just get to the pharmacy first, drop off the prescription, and then come back for her while they are filling it? You know I have a busy day." The voice said, "Pick her up now!"

So, I turned around in the first driveway I came to and pulled up beside her. I rolled down my window and asked, "Would you like a ride home?" She said, "I had just been praying for help. I feel like I may faint soon. I didn't know it was this hot when I decided to walk to the store."

She got in my car and I took her home. She lived on my street, but we had never met. She was very grateful.

A few months later, I walked past her house which had a "garage sale" sign on display in the front yard. I stopped in to see how the lady was doing. I talked to her daughter, and found out that the older woman had just died. I told the lady about my encounter with her mother. I was so grateful to God for the grace to help her when I did.

God's Call to Action

Amy Hartig

A voice in my head has been with me through most of my adult life. Usually, it is just little nudges here and there to extend kindness to someone or to make a decision for me or my family. Sometimes it seems that I'm just in the right place at the right time to provide gas for a desperate woman or food to a homeless man, etc.

My work with St. Vincent de Paul[28] has provided me with many of these moments. I find that in these situations I receive a bountiful gift of Grace. I feel pure love and joy that refuels me for the next challenge!

Here are two examples:

Each year, as I interview families for our St. Vincent de Paul Christmas program, there are always a couple of situations in which I feel called to provide help beyond the usual Christmas needs of food and gifts.

One year, we had a family who was living in our area because their daughter was being treated at the local Children's Hospital. As I asked about the family's needs for Christmas, the mother explained their current situation. They had arrived several months before with nothing but the clothes on their back. They had not planned to stay, but the hospital encouraged them to remain in town. Now they were about to lose all of their belongings in a three-bedroom rental home in South Carolina. The mother had no funds left to meet the family's needs, and her parents were ill. As I hung up the phone my husband looked at me and said, "I guess we are going South Carolina!"

With the support of our St. Vincent de Paul Conference President, my husband and I drove a truck to the family's former home in South Carolina. The mother had already recruited a friend and local church members to pack up the contents of the house. Once the truck was loaded, they prayed over us, and we headed back home.

We had contacted our local Christ Renews His Parish[4] friends to help us move the family's belongings from the truck into their home here. The mother was so grateful and couldn't believe folks from a different faith would help in such a way. Several years later, we coordinated with our Christ Renews His Parish friends again, to help pack their belongings when she was ready to move back to South Carolina.

> *"For our light and momentary troubles are achieving for us an eternal glory that far outweighs them all."* 2 Corinthians 4:17

While contacting families for our St. Vincent de Paul program, I received a call from a woman we had served in the past. Her husband had never fully recovered from COVID, and they were struggling with all aspects of their lives. Not only did she need assistance with Christmas, but they needed help with all of their bills. They were in jeopardy of eviction and disconnection of their utilities.

Since their needs were beyond that of our conference funds, I helped her with the Healthy at Home Emergency Relief Fund[9] application. I prayed with her and encouraged her, as this process takes some time. I escalated the case when she received her first eviction notice. I said rosaries for her and prayed as she attended her court hearing. As Christmas approached, we kept in contact via phone calls and text messages. We prayed together and I was certain God would answer our prayers.

Unfortunately, they were evicted right before Christmas. I was feeling her despair myself, as she was also suffering from a recent death in her family. We kept praying together and God kept providing me with encouraging words for her. It wasn't until after Christmas, when she thanked me for helping her through this difficult time, that

I realized that had been His plan! She had just needed emotional and spiritual support to get through all of her challenges.

Now they are in a better home than they had been before! I thank God for this lesson. We both learned to trust in God and persist in prayer.

"It is the Holy Spirit to whom those precious impulses are due. Daily, every hour, He is knocking at our hearts, speaking to us, drawing us. One of the truest ways we may learn of His presence is when he calls our attention to some good work and encourages us to do it."
Father Thomas Augustine Judge (1868–1933)

"Come Out of the Water!"

Claire Patterson

After writing Through Mary's Eyes, it was suggested that I write a second book about our experiences in Medjugorje. I never considered this request seriously, because I was skeptical that anyone would care to read about my story. If I'm really being honest, I was also selfish and lazy. I didn't want to invest the time or the money that writing, editing, and publishing a book requires.

In August of 2020 I took my granddaughter to Virginia Beach for a short vacation. While sitting in my chair on the sand, I began reading a book about Our Lady of Light[19] while Ella was swimming in the ocean. A voice in my heart said, "Go home and write a book about your conversion story."

I called my granddaughter out of the water and said, "We have to go home. God is telling me to write another book. I can't wait to begin!"

Once God asked me to do it, I jumped right into the process. I wrote Finding Grace Through Mary's Eyes in about six weeks!

> *"...I have never heard Him speak, and yet I know He is within my soul. Every moment He is guiding me and inspiring me, and just at the moment I need them, lights, till then unseen, are granted me..."* St. Therese of Lisieux, The Story of a Soul

Trying to Hide Jesus

Claire Patterson

One of my favorite stories about Pope St. John Paul II[26] involves the still small voice that he heard one day during his travels. One of his aides tells this story:

The Pope and his retinue were behind schedule more than usual. St. John Paul II liked to stop in Adoration Chapels[1] wherever he visited, but on this particular day, the aide felt there just wouldn't be enough time for the Pontiff to do so.

The aide called ahead and asked the local coordinator to hide all signs inside and outside of the building that would direct visitors to the Adoration Chapel. He also suggested that the door of the chapel be disguised, so that the Pope would not recognize it as an Adoration Chapel.

As the group passed the door to the chapel the Pope paused, looked at his aide, and wagged his finger in reprimand. He then turned around, opened the door, and entered for a nice visit with Jesus. It's almost as if Jesus was calling, "Karol, Karol, stop in and visit with Me." And he did just that!

God Saves

Joe Gering

In June of 1972 I was in the Army stationed outside of Seoul, South Korea. I was assigned for a six-week period to Camp Howard for Dog Handler Duty. As it turned out, it seemed to me that Camp Howard was a den of iniquity and corruption.

One day, I approached the E-7 Sergeant in charge of the Military Police and Dog Handlers School at Camp Howard concerning my observations. He became very upset and warned me about the trouble that I could be in for questioning him. His assistant, an E-6 Sergeant, tried to get me to back off. He admitted that the E-7 was running some "black market" operations and an "extortion racket". He also told me that if I didn't mind my own business, I might end up dead out in the field. I was also threatened with a court martial for insubordination.

One weekend I went back to our home base and told our Base Commander and Section Chief about the alarming issues. They made the two-hour drive to Camp Howard the next day to talk with the E-7 Sergeant. They let him know that they were monitoring the situation very closely, and if anything were to happen to me, they would launch an investigation.

Things calmed down a bit until the end of my six weeks at Camp Howard. In addition to myself, there were about ten or twelve others who were assigned there for the same temporary duty. We were all invited to a party on the Camp Howard main post. Several men stationed there were invited as well. I became concerned when the beer began to flow freely. Some of the temporaries, like me, did not always get along with some of the main-stays during our six weeks of special training.

Sure enough, we weren't at the party long before I sensed the mood beginning to change. Something or someone was telling me that it was time to leave. So, my friend and I left the party and went to the movie house for two hours. When we returned to the party room, everyone was gone and the place was in shambles. We went to our barracks and discovered that the Military Police had come and beaten up and arrested several of the guys at the party. They told me that the MPs were specifically looking for me!

God showed me, in so many ways, that I was under His protection.

In March 1973, I was asked to take on the responsibilities of a Duty Driver on a temporary basis until a new one could arrive at our home base.

One night I had to drive a two-and-a half ton Army truck to get parts for our Missile Site protecting Seoul. I was assigned a good assistant to accompany me on the five-hour trip.

It was raining all night and the fog was very thick. I could only drive five to fifteen miles per hour on the winding, slick mountain roads. It was very difficult to see. As we were creeping along, I had this feeling that I needed to stop – right now! There was no real reason, it was just this feeling. I couldn't explain it.

As I stopped, there was a slight break in the fog for a couple seconds. I saw a woman and three little children standing frozen in the middle of the road! They didn't know whether to try to make it across, or try to get back. My friend exclaimed, "Joe, how did you see them?" I told him, "I didn't see them. Something just kept telling me to stop."

Our Heavenly Father always has a plan if we would only listen and respond to it.

CHAPTER 3

God Extends Invitations

"In all simplicity, I believe that Jesus Himself is, in a mysterious way, at work in the depths of my soul, inspiring me with whatever He wants me to do at that moment."
St. Therese of Lisieux - The Story of a Soul

Invitation to a Pilgrimage

Claire Patterson

I was helping with a three-day mission during Lent in 2017 when an acquaintance began to walk into the church. I called out, "Hello, Sheila." She turned around quickly and said, "Claire, I am so glad I ran into you. I have been wanting to talk to you but didn't have your phone number. I am looking for someone to travel with me to Medjugorje[11] in September. Will you go with me?"

The Holy Spirit inspired me to say, "Yes" immediately. That week we began to make plans for the trip. She invited another friend, Alice, about a month later. I met a friend, Peggy, in the parking lot of our church after Mass one day, and the Holy Spirit urged me to tell her about our planned trip. She decided she wanted to go with us; so, then we were four.

This trip was wonderful and challenging in many ways.

Our Spiritual Director was Immaculee Ilibagiza. Before leaving the U.S., I had received a call from Immaculee's assistant to find their friend, Valentine Nyiramukiza, at the airport in Croatia, and make sure she boarded the bus taking us all to Medjugorje. (Valentine is one of the Kibeho, Rwandan visionaries and does not speak English or Croatian. We managed to communicate through informal sign language.)

We were so privileged to spend a week with these two holy women. Our local guide was Micky Musso, who is also very dedicated to our Lord and our Blessed Mother.

One of the nicest aspects of our time in Medjugorje was being able to find each other, Immaculee, Micky, or Valentine, whenever it was necessary. In a town filled with thousands of pilgrims, we could almost feel our guardian angels taking us by the hand to guide us where we needed to be.

Peggy fell while climbing down Apparition Hill, during our first full day there. I was right in front of her, but couldn't stop her tumble. She scraped her leg badly, and she hit her back on a rock. (She found out when she returned home that she had fractured a vertebra.) By the Grace of God, there was a group of Polish pilgrims nearby, and they rushed over to help.

One of them was an English-speaking nurse. She began treating Peggy for shock, and directing several strong men to carry her carefully. In the meantime, I rushed to the bottom of the hill and flagged a taxi. I threw some money at the driver, asking him to wait for Peg to come down. The men brought her down the hill carefully, following the directions of the Polish nurse. Then the taxi rushed Peggy and Sheila to the first-aid station near St. James' Church. The medics cleaned her leg wounds but could do nothing for her back, since they did not have an x-ray machine, to determine the damage to her spine and the extent of her injuries.

Unfortunately for Peggy, she was bed-ridden for much of the rest of the week. One night, during an apparition with Ivan Dragicevic, one of the six visionaries, I was with Peg in our room. I opened our window which faced the Apparition Hill[2]. Miraculously, we could hear everything going on before, during and after Our Blessed Mother's visit. When comparing notes with the other pilgrims who had been on the Hill during the apparition, we discovered that we had heard everything even more clearly than those who had been closer to Ivan!

(Note: see Chapter 8, "Don't You Trust Me?" for Peggy's memories of the event.)

A Special Christmas Gift

M. A. B.

In 1998 my brother sent a book to me for Christmas. We don't usually exchange gifts so I was surprised to receive it. It was a book about the Virgin Mary's apparitions around the world. My faith was not very strong at that time, so I set the book aside for about six months. When I finally got around to reading it, I started crying. I cried a lot. That really jump-started my interest in Mary and how she speaks to the most average of people.

A few weeks later there was an announcement at Mass encouraging us to sign up for a Christ Renews His Parish[4] weekend. I had always ignored these appeals because I'm not a "joiner." This particular day, however, I had a strong and overwhelming urge to add my name to the list. Unfortunately, that fervor didn't last as the weekend approached. I was really kicking myself for having committed to it. Nevertheless, I attended and was amazed and overwhelmed by the variety of women and their stories. We were all on a faith journey but at different places along the road, with some very different narratives.

I had made a deal with God that I would go to the weekend, but only if He'd make sure I didn't cry in front of others. Needless to say, I cried a lot that weekend and some of the women I met are still my friends today. One happy outcome of these friendships was belonging to a wonderful rosary group that became a very important part of my life. I'm so glad I received that Christmas gift from my brother.

The Lady Praying From Her Heart

Claire Patterson

After Duke died, I began to think about selling our house. I was happy with my prayer walks, friends at church, and Duke's gardens, but I felt a need to live closer to my daughter and her family. I was also becoming aware that the neighborhood in which I lived was no longer as safe as it once had been. My daughter and her husband had mentioned a few times that they no longer felt comfortable with me living there. Furthermore, it was becoming difficult for me to maintain the gardens, shovel the snow, and cut the grass. Worse yet, my parish had just been merged with two other parishes, and they all shared one priest; daily Mass had been reduced to only two per week.

In April 2015 I happily moved into my low-maintenance condominium. I searched on the internet for Roman Catholic Parishes nearby and the name "Blessed Sacrament Church" popped up. I got excited when I read that the parish had two Masses **each day** with two priests and a deacon. They also had a thriving school, and I love attending the children's Masses. I also discovered that, prior to the ten-o'clock daily Mass, there is a Rosary said by the early attendees. I was very happy to join this parish.

It's funny, but you never know the value of a moment until it becomes a memory.

One of the first times I attended the pre-Mass Rosary, I sensed that the woman leading the rosary was praying humbly from her heart. This woman was following one of Mary's requests we had learned from the beginning of our experiences in 2001: "Pray, pray, pray, especially from your heart, especially the Rosary."

I also heard that still small voice from God nudging me to find that lady after the Mass and give her a copy of Through Mary's Eyes, a book I had published in 2011.

So, even though I was uncomfortable approaching her, I did what I felt God wanted me to do. By listening to God's whisper, this small gesture opened the door to so many other connections with the faithful people of our community. This special lady, Pat, very quickly, introduced me to many of her faith-filled friends. I was invited to join a Blessed Sacrament Rosary group, the "Respect-for-Life" committee, Bible study, the Spiritual Motherhood of Priests, and Holy Hour each week in a nearby Adoration Chapel[1]. By the way, Pat is the artist for this book!

A few months later, I felt God encouraging me to give my book to "the tall blonde lady" who attended 10:00 a.m. Holy Mass most days of the week. Since it was Christmas time, I wrapped the book in holiday paper and said simply, "God wants you to have this book." By following God's will, I was introduced to yet another dear friend, Julie, and subsequently, the "Walking with Purpose"[29] group, and many other affiliations with Blessed Sacrament Parish.

(Note: See Chapter 8, "Will You Suffer for Me?" for Julie's story.)

I feel very blessed to have found so many devout friends among the community in which I now live. My faith continues to deepen with these amazing and inspiring women.

Thank you, God, for guiding me every step of the way.

"...the Lord looks into the heart." 1 Samuel 16:7

From a 'Sunday' Catholic to an 'Every Day' Catholic

Bob Smaracko

I was raised Catholic and served as an altar boy from my youth until my senior year in high school. I had thoughts about becoming a priest, yet that changed when I began to notice and became interested in women and beer.

In 1989, I married Trish. We were both thirty-three years young at the time of our wedding. While I did not directly request it, Trish converted to Catholicism prior to our marriage. We welcomed our son, Michael, into this world in 1996.

I was, and still am, a member of the Holy Name Society (HNS). One of HNS's important projects is organizing and facilitating the delivery of the annual men's Christ Renews His Parish (CRHP) retreat[4]. A CRHP retreat is a two-day event starting early on a Saturday morning and ending in the afternoon on Sunday. The participants spend the night at the facility where the retreat is being conducted. What's said and discussed at CRHP stays at CRHP.

Every year, I would be approached by men involved with CRHP who would encourage me to participate in the retreat. My response was usually, "I'm already very close to God and a devout Catholic. There is little that I can learn. I probably could teach you about being closer to our Lord." That attitude prevailed for more than ten years.

From 2009 to 2012 I found myself in a few unrewarding, uninspiring jobs. For the first time in my life, it was difficult to get out of bed. I would take Michael to school and return home to wallow in my grief.

The distance between Trish and me grew wider and I became less involved in Michael's life and activities. Most nights I wouldn't even join them for a family dinner, as I was in the lower level consumed with internet surfing and drinking beer. Michael refers to that time as the "dark days" of my life.

Meanwhile, Trish had been screaming for help to resolve our differences and to restore the glory days of our marriage. Her attempts to heal our marriage included a Retrouville retreat and numerous counseling sessions. However, I was so confident that our marriage would last a lifetime, that I simply ignored Trish's cries for help. I had been aloof and unaware of her true feelings and the emotional wounds that I had inflicted upon her. My life was always focused on me. I treated my customers better than I treated Trish!

In 2012, I had returned from a business trip and found a note on the kitchen counter. Trish stated that she was leaving me. She had had her fill of my emotionally hurtful and selfish actions over the years. I had believed that there was no way that Trish was actually going to leave me and Michael. Regrettably, I learned otherwise.

In 2013, thanks to a long-time friend, I landed a great position with a good company. With this positive turn in my professional life, my alcohol consumption was significantly reduced. I was excited, once again, about "hitting it" each and every morning.

I tried to make amends with Trish, yet she was adamant about pursuing a separation. Frankly, I didn't blame her. The reality is that we had grown quite distant from one another relative to our political, religious and social beliefs.

In 2016, Deacon Larry was in charge of the delivery of the Christ Renews His Parish weekend for our parish. Larry and I were pretty good friends, so he pestered me for weeks to participate in the retreat. I told Deacon Larry the same thing that I had told my friends for years; "A CRHP retreat would be a waste of my time."

Deacon Larry was relentless in his recruiting pursuits. One Sunday, he approached me again and said, "I'll bet you ten dollars that if you participate in our CRHP retreat, your life will be changed forever." Well, in the interest of appeasing Deacon Larry and to stop his nagging, I relented and agreed to attend the CRHP retreat. Heck, this was going to be the easiest ten dollars I would ever make!

I was so confident that I was going to stay for an hour, leave and collect my ten dollars from Deacon Larry, that I didn't even pack an overnight bag!

During the retreat weekend, the team shared their individual and intimate experiences and details of some of their life situations. Their presentations focused on an array of topics including addiction (alcohol, drugs, gambling, pornography), divorce, obsession with money, mental and emotional effects of spousal and family abuse, as well as their departure from, and return to, the Catholic faith.

Following each presentation, we would have a table discussion relative to the presenter's story and, tearfully share our own experiences with related predicaments.

All of the presentations were captivating and heart-wrenching. Many of the men broke down into tears as they shared their stories. Many of us retreatants also shed tears as we reflected upon our lives and our own personal experiences relative to the presenter's message.

The next thing I knew, it was lunchtime. Wait …….lunch time?!?!?!? I had planned to only stay an hour!!!! I had become so consumed by the presentations and table discussions that I had lost all track of time. It's amazing how the Good Lord operates by leading us on a path to insight and redemption; if we only open our eyes, ears, soul, heart and mind to Him.

Throughout the weekend there was ample time for table and one-on-one discussions, personal reflection, recitation of the rosary, confession, Mass and Adoration. Honestly, other than going to Mass, I couldn't remember the last time that I had participated in many of these holy activities.

My CRHP confession was especially rewarding for me, as it allowed me to unload years of sinful activity and thoughts. Following confession, I found myself in a state of inner peace; almost in a state of euphoria. I was confident that the Lord had forgiven all of my past transgressions. I began to feel the sensation of a spiritual high; something that I had never experienced in my life.

Sunday morning was soon upon us. (And yes, I did go back to my home Saturday evening to pack some overnight things.) The retreat concluded mid-Sunday afternoon with Mass. The spiritual high that I mentioned was becoming more and more intense.

I got into my car to head home, but something strange occurred. As I was sitting in my car in the church parking lot, I became acutely focused on the large cross atop the church. I didn't want to go home; I didn't want my CRHP experience to end!!!! This couldn't be!!!! I recalled all of the years that I did and said anything and everything to avoid attending a CRHP retreat. What the heck was going on?!?!?!

For the remainder of Sunday afternoon and over the course of the next several weeks, my spiritual high continued to be most profound.

Now, each day begins with prayer, thanking the Lord for my life and the many gifts He has bestowed upon me. I also ask the Lord to teach me how to pray and to be my coach and my guide throughout the day. I pray for family members and friends who are in need of prayer.

In the weeks following CRHP, I approached Deacon Larry and offered to pay the ten dollars I owed him. Respectfully, and not surprisingly, Deacon Larry simply smiled and motioned for me to put the money back in my pocket. In his heart, he knew that he had *won* our bet. Praise the Lord and give thanks to Deacon Larry for his persistence in bringing me to this new chapter in my life.

I humbly submit the following chart of my life's actions pre-CRHP and post-CRHP. It is not all inclusive, yet represents many habits of my life which are new actions; others are clearly improvements as a result of my participation in CRHP.

Activity	Pre-CRHP	Post-CRHP
Adoration[1]	Never	1 – 2 times per week
Attendance at daily Mass	Never	3 – 4 times per week
Vulgar language, obscene jokes and unkind thoughts, words and actions	Often	Short of mental lapses, I have eliminated vulgar language from my vocabulary and thoughts; obscene jokes are a thing of the past. I focus on awareness of my actions, thoughts and words.
Frequent Confession	I couldn't recall the last time I went to Confession	My goal is monthly Confession. I do pretty well hitting this goal.
Daily Recitation of the Rosary	No way – it took too long	Every day, and sometimes multiple rosaries per day.
Bible study	Never	This is a target area of improvement and focus for me. Bible = Basic Instructions Before Leaving Earth

Activity	Pre-CRHP	Post-CRHP
Daily Prayer	Nope	Yes, every day, multiple times during the day. God is everywhere. I pray in the car, while on the treadmill… anywhere and often.
Daily Prayer to my Guardian Angel	No way	I have given my Guardian Angel the name of Pio. Each day I ask Pio to guide my actions, thoughts and words.
Listening to Catholic Radio	No way – too boring	Yes
Intense focus on money	Yes!!!	The Lord will provide for me and I will provide for those in need.
Focus on the value of family	Kinda'	I regret that it took me so long to truly understand the importance and value of family relationships.
Complete surrender to, trust in, and acceptance of God's will for me	No way …….why would I do that?	Yes. Life is much easier when we succumb to our Lord's will for us. I now "Let go and let God." As Padre Pio[25] says: "Don't worry. Be happy! Trust in the Lord!"

Our good Lord knows what is best for all of us and has a plan for each of us. It is not our prerogative to question any situation that He presents to us, yet rather, learn from it. I realize that this is, at times, very frustrating and difficult, yet surrendering to God brings peace.

As the saying goes: "If I knew then what I know now, how different my life would be."

Note: Robert Smaracko took his last breath on September 22, 2023, on the eve of the feast of St. Pius of Pietrelcina (Padre Pio). Bob was a co-founder of the Padre Pio prayer group in Northern Kentucky. May he rest in peace.

"In this you rejoice, although now for a little while you may have to suffer through various trials, so that the genuineness of your faith, ***more precious than gold*** *that is perishable even though tested by fire, may prove to be for praise, glory and honor at the revelation of Jesus Christ."* 1 Peter 1:6-7

CHAPTER 4

A Whisper to Help or Heal

Madeline

Claire Patterson

In 2000 my church asked us to spiritually adopt an unborn child who was in danger of being aborted. After Holy Mass one day, I heard a whisper telling me to go up to the altar and write the name, "Madeline," into the book assigned to record the names of the unborn babies for which we were praying. I began asking God, each day, to spare Madeline's life.

A few months later, I was alone in the lunch room of the building in which I was working. A man came in and stood by the doorway, talking on his cell phone. At one point during his conversation, I overheard him say, "Well, Dad, you're going to be a grandfather. We thought about aborting the baby, but decided to keep it. We just found out it will be a girl, and we are going to name her Madeline."

You can imagine my joy! I thanked God profusely, not only for saving Madeline's life, but for allowing me to become aware of another unborn life saved from abortion. This event also reaffirmed my belief in the power of prayer.

"Visit Ilsa"

M. A. B.

For several years I took Communion to some home-bound people. One of them was an elderly woman who lived alone and didn't have any family nearby. One week she hadn't been feeling well while I was there, so I made sure she had all the food that she needed. She assured me she'd be fine.

While my husband and I were out running errands the next day, I told him we needed to visit Ilse. I had no reason to suspect anything was wrong; I just knew I had to check in on her.

When we arrived at her home, the neighbor who cuts her grass was outside. He informed me that he'd yelled through the door to her when he had arrived and she had answered him. He assured me that she was fine. Nevertheless, I felt strongly that I had to go inside to see her. When I entered her bedroom, I didn't see her immediately. I found her on the floor where she had fallen. She was also very confused and didn't know where she was. I called an ambulance for her and the medics said they thought she had been on the floor for quite a while. It turned out she was very sick.

I always listen to those "still, small voices." They've never been wrong.

"I have told you this so that you may have peace in Me.
In the world you will have trouble, but take courage,
I have conquered the world." John 16:33

A Walk Together

Anonymous

As a deacon, I am privileged to visit people who are homebound due to sickness or other issues. There was one woman, named Edna, who had terminal liver cancer. I visited her each week, gave her Holy Communion, and we reminisced about our lives. Edna had a great sense of humor and a true love for all of her family members.

One evening, I received a call from her neighbor that the end of Edna's life was close. I was at a soccer game for my grandson, and I left immediately, and drove to her house.

When I arrived, the house was full of friends and relatives. Since I knew where she would be, I entered her room and saw that people were standing at the far end of the room, away from her bed. I walked over, held her hand, and stroked her hair. She opened her eyes, then closed them and died.

A number of people came over and told me that she had been waiting for me to come. My response was that she just needed someone to hold her hand as she walked toward her heavenly home.

"The Lord is my shepherd; there is nothing I lack. In green pastures you let me graze; to safe waters you lead me; You restore my strength. You guide me along the right path for the sake of Your name. Even when I walk through a dark valley, I fear no harm for You are at my side; Your rod and staff give me courage." Psalm 23:1-4

The HVAC Guy

Claire Patterson

In May 2013, I was having regular maintenance performed on my air conditioning and heating units. As the serviceman was working on my systems, I sensed a whisper in my heart encouraging me to give him a copy of Through Mary's Eyes. I felt uncomfortable offering it to him, with no clue as to his religious affiliation or whether he even believed in God. He simply said, "Thank you," and took it with him when he left.

Six months later, during his next routine visit, he told me that he had read the book and shared it with his sister. He told me that they had both left their church years before, but the book gave them the encouragement they needed to return to God. He was so grateful that I had given him a copy of Through Mary's Eyes.

I was thankful that God gave me the nudge to get out of my comfort zone, and the courage to share the book with a stranger.

"Fashionista, Give it Away"

Alicia Brocker

The Three Amigos! That's what we call ourselves; two of my very best friends and me!

We LOVE fashion; anything from high-end designers to budget fashion, and everything in between! We love it all! If we see something online that we know the other will love, we will link it to our group chat with the caption, "You need this!" We all have very different styles: Classy, Sexy, Cool- that almost sounds like a TLC album! (All my 80's-90's friends will get that reference!) And we love and appreciate each other's unique sense of style. Lovingly, we will often encourage one of us to step out of her box. We have the best time with fashion!

In my opinion, there's nothing wrong in taking delight in fashion. The worthy wife is referenced multiple times in the Bible, regarding her selecting fabrics, making clothes, and dressing in fine linen and purple.

"She obtains wool and flax and makes cloth with skillful hands. Like merchant ships she secures her provisions from afar...she puts her hands to the distaff, and her fingers ply the spindle...she makes her own coverlets; fine linen and purple are her clothing..." Proverbs 31:13-14, 19, 22

She liked to look nice too! I always aspire to be like that Proverbs 31 woman. I'm so glad she loved fashion and looking well-dressed as much as I do! I'm blessed and grateful that I have a healthy relationship with fashion now, but it wasn't always that way for me.

Let me explain.

Since I was a little girl, I have been captivated by fashion. I loved going shopping and always had a great eye for color and design. I was just eighteen years old when I entered the hair industry, and a whole new level of fashion was introduced to me. The women and men stylists knew how to dress, to be sure, and it wowed me! I learned all about the high-end designers as we trekked down the Magnificent Mile in Chicago, and made visits to Saks 5th Avenue in Cincinnati.

The elitism and expense of these luxury items enticed me - I had to have them! I wanted all the Bebe. (It was the early 2000's after all!) I wanted the Graffiti Louis Vuitton purses, Burberry bikinis and all the other hot new trends! I was single, worked hard, with few expenses at the time, and so, I let myself indulge in these luxuries!

However, sometimes our love for things can overcome us. We can become so consumed by it, that it starts to rob us of our identity in Christ. The short happiness is fleeting, and we're left feeling empty again, and insecure. Addiction takes over, so we feel the need for more and more gratification. If we are not careful, our vanity and pride could replace our need for God. I became that glutton for stuff, and was sliding down a slippery slope.

I'm grateful to the Holy Spirit for a much-needed intervention! I had just met my future husband at that time, and he was the cup of cool water that I needed. He was a down-to-earth Christian, and although he liked nice things too, he wasn't above wearing a thrift store vintage find.

During those first few months of dating, I journaled a lot. I prayed a lot. God was stirring something in me that was well overdue.

I knew I needed to let go of the things I thought defined me. I remember the Holy Spirit convicting my heart to "give it away" if I could. This was hard for me. If someone were to compliment me on something I was wearing or owned, if I could take it off modestly, I should give it to them! That's what I was supposed to do! It was so clear, but it scared the heck out of me. I loved my stuff!

I remember one occasion clearly. I had just recently purchased a Louis Vuitton makeup bag from another stylist. It was gorgeous! It was yellow Epi leather with a purple interior! I was at my work station and had it out, applying my lipstick after lunch when another, newer stylist, complimented me on it. "Oh my gosh! I LOVE your makeup bag!" she said enthusiastically.

Well, you can guess what happened next: I looked at her, smiled, and dumped the contents into my purse and handed the makeup bag over to her. Shocked, she said, "Are you serious? You're GIVING this to me?" And I said, "Yep! You're meant to have it."

I thought it would be painful to give my things away, but for the first time, in a long time, it felt so freeing! It was much more rewarding to bless someone else rather than being self-indulgent.

On another occasion, I was traveling somewhere with one of my best friends, and I was wearing an expensive butterfly choker from Bebe. We were in the backseat of someone's car when she said, "I love your necklace! It's so cool!" Immediately, I took it off and gave it to her. "It's yours!," I said. She was shocked. "What!? That's awesome! Oh my gosh! Thank you so much!" she said, as she graciously accepted my gift.

This gifting pattern didn't last too long, but just long enough to break some bonds of coveting, materialism and vanity; all the things that had been keeping me from Christ. Praying to be humble is a scary but necessary prayer at times. It took a decade or two before I found my appropriate balance with fashion again.

"Everything is lawful for me, but not everything is beneficial. Everything is lawful for me, but I will not let myself be dominated by anything."
1 Corinthians 6:12

Love Always

Anonymous

When my son was very involved with drugs, I didn't even want to be in the same room with him. He had been lying to my wife and me, and stealing from our family. We had a big argument one day and I went to bed very angry with him.

In the middle of the night, I heard a voice say to me, "The time to love your child the most, is when you don't like him."

I went immediately into my son's room and hugged him as he fought against my hug. I told him I would always love him.

Through my prayers, and the prayers of many others, and God's grace, he is drug-free as I write this story.

Feed the Hungry

Claire Patterson

In 1974 I was not praying often enough, nor was I keeping my soul pure.

I had just picked up a couple of pieces of Kentucky Fried Chicken for my dinner. This was a rare treat for me, as I didn't have much money back then, and it was my favorite meal.

As I left the KFC, I passed a rough-looking man going through the trash cans outside of the restaurant. I kept walking, a little afraid of him.

I felt the Holy Spirit inviting me to give him my meal. I kept walking away. When I got home, I couldn't enjoy my food.

All these years later, I still regret that act of selfishness. I had other food at home I could have eaten. He probably didn't even have a home to go to.

God, please forgive me!

"The kindly man will be blessed, for he gives of his sustenance to the poor." Proverbs 22:9

God Guides a Mom

Joe Gering

I was about eight months old in 1951. I had gotten a cold and was having difficulty breathing. My parents took me to the hospital. The medical staff immediately put me into an oxygen tent while they were considering performing a tracheotomy on me. Mom never left the room.

Soon, she noticed that I was struggling even harder to breathe. She pulled me out of the tent and called the nurse. They discovered that the equipment hadn't been turned on. If Mom hadn't stayed right with me, I wouldn't be here today.

No doubt, Divine Providence was guiding my Mom.

Sleeping In

Joan McGranahan

My husband left for work one Sunday morning in 1992. After he left, I decided to go back to bed, sleep in, and not attend Mass. My conscience was making it very hard to roll over and close my eyes again, but I kept trying.

Then the phone rang at 9:45 a.m. It was Sister Mary Phillip, who was assigned to our parish. She explained that her legs were hurting that morning and she was scheduled to be a Eucharistic Minister[7] for the 10:30 a.m. Mass. It was during Lent and our Pastor requested that all the ministers kneel at the foot of the altar for a few minutes before going up to the altar. Sister didn't think she could do that because of the pain in her legs, so she asked if I would fill in. Of course, no one ever says "NO" to a nun, so, I told her I would be happy to fill in.

I had to rush to get dressed so I could make it on time. All the way to church I kept telling God that I would not think about missing Mass intentionally ever again.

After Mass I told Sister Mary Phillip my story and she said that I was the only person she could think of to call and help her out. I know that God used her to get me out of bed and to church. I told her she must have a direct line to God.

Sister Mary Philip heard and obeyed "that still small voice" and in doing so, helped me grow closer to God. I have never considered skipping Mass again!

A St. Michael Statue

Anonymous

I had wanted a nice statue of St. Michael the Archangel for a long time; ever since my devotion to him had begun to grow. I finally splurged and bought one in a local gift shop one weekday morning, and took it to church to have it blessed before our 10:00 a.m. Mass. I found our priest praying in a pew.

After he finished his prayers, I asked him to bless my statue. While he was blessing it, I felt God wanted him to have the statue.

I asked, "Father, do you have a statue of St. Michael?" He said, "No." I said, "Then, this one is yours." It was still in the box and bag from the gift shop. He seemed very pleased to have it.

I pray for all of our priests, every day, as I know they are under constant attack from Satan, and St. Michael is always a great help.

God Whispers to a Mother

M. A. B.

One sleepy weekend morning, I was drinking coffee in the kitchen. I'm not a morning person, so I was content just to sit quietly. My six-year-old daughter came and proudly showed me that she had lost a tooth. She was quite excited and happy about it. I think there was some talk about the tooth fairy. She went into the bathroom to look at the "hole" left by the lost tooth, when I had a very strong urge to follow her. I just felt that I needed to go in there — NOW! I walked into the bathroom just in time to catch her as she fainted.

When that same daughter was about thirteen years old, she was having some female issues. I had taken her to the doctor who said she'd be fine.

I have three kids and had never spent the night sleeping in one of their rooms, but that night I had the feeling that I needed to sleep in her room with her.

During the night she got up to use the bathroom and I just knew I had to follow her. I walked a few steps behind her and caught her as she was passing out. We called an ambulance for her and she was in the hospital for a couple of days.

I'm so grateful that I listened to that voice that encouraged me to sleep in her room.

"You have tested my heart, searched it in the night. You have tried me by fire, but find no malice in me." Psalm 17:3

A Hat from Santa

Anonymous

In mid-December, on a bitterly cold morning, I was in church early for the 10:00 a.m. Mass. The priest, who was scheduled to say Mass, walked in quickly. He was practically bald and had nothing on his head. A voice in my heart told me, "Buy my Shepherd a hat."

So, after Mass, I drove to the mall. The large department store I had planned to visit was closed, but I found a smaller boutique store close-by with a parking spot – open! (A rare event that close to Christmas!) I trusted in God that they would have men's hats, and they had two varieties - on sale!

I bought one, brought it home and put it in a Christmas bag with festive tissue paper. The next morning, I arrived very early to church, and left it in the sacristy with the Priest's name on the bag's tag. I told the Sacristan, who caught me in the act, to tell Father that it was a gift from "Santa."

It warmed my heart, when a couple of days later, I watched God's Shepherd putting on the hat as he headed out of church into the bitter cold.

God is good! He always cares for me, and when I open my heart, and listen to His voice, He can use me to aid others.

A New Kidney

A. T.

I had worked with Tracy for many years, but only as casual colleagues. I knew she had some medical issues, but I wasn't aware of the exact problem. So, I would pray for her, but I never said anything to her about her health.

After I retired in October of 2017, I learned that Tracy needed a new kidney. I then prayed specifically, "Lord, please let someone donate a kidney to her."

In March of 2018, Tracy created a Facebook post describing her need for a kidney. She included the business card of a nurse-coordinator who would test for a match if someone was willing to donate their kidney. I happened to see the post and got scared. I just scrolled away thinking, "Not me!"

I prayed daily for her to find a donor. In prayer I sensed that God was asking me to give her my kidney. I ignored the feeling for two months, as I thought, "Oh, someone in her family will do it. I'm not even close to her. I haven't seen her or talked to her since I retired."

That nudge from God did not go away. I prayed, "Lord do you really want me to give her my kidney?" So, in May I searched Facebook for her old post and called the nurse-coordinator thinking, "If it's God's will, then I will be a match for her. But hopefully, someone else has already agreed to donate to her."

After asking me many medical questions, the nurse-coordinator sent the paperwork to me to get a blood test. What do you know? I was a match for Tracy!

I had to text another coworker to get Tracy's phone number. When we connected, she was so excited!

I asked my Christ Renews His Parish[4] sisters to pray a novena to St. Therese for a successful surgery for Tracy and me, scheduled for October 1, 2018[27].

Tracy's new kidney is working well for her and I'm trying to listen to God's voice each day and follow His will.

CHAPTER 5

An Infusion of Knowledge

"For the Lord gives wisdom, from His mouth
come knowledge and understanding."
Proverbs 2:6

A Lesson Learned at the Festival

Donna Allen

I grew up in the 60's as a cradle Catholic. We learned – no memorized - the Baltimore Catechism in school. We went to Mass every Wednesday, wearing napkins on our heads, if we had forgotten our chapel veils.

As a family, we were "Chreasters." I remember getting dressed up in the awful matching dresses my mom made for my sister and me and going to Mass as a family on Christmas and Easter, but I don't recall that Sunday Mass was a big deal throughout the rest of the year.

As I reflect on "God moments" in my early life, there is one that I definitely did not recognize as such until decades later, but it is a moment that has remained in my heart all these years.

My Dad and I were at the St. Mary's Parish festival. I was around six or seven years old. I was playing a game where you put money on a number, and when the wheel spins, the winning number wins all the dough. I put my quarter on a number and the wheel landed on the number next to mine. When the spinner's back was toward me, I shifted my quarter to the winning number's slot and – bam! – won the money! No one suspected a thing. Woo Hoo!

When I quickly left the booth, so as not to draw suspicion, I found myself bursting into tears. I sought out my dad as I cried uncontrollably. He asked what was wrong, and I told him what I had done. He very calmly said, "Let's go back there and spend all your winnings on the game, therefore returning all the money back to the booth, and the parish." And that's what we did.

Now, you're thinking, "That's it? Shouldn't he have scolded you or made an example of your bad behavior? Shouldn't he have narc'd you out to the Festival Committee?"

But, no. My dad saw that I was remorseful, and that I had already recognized the fault in my choice. So, by his response, he taught me, without saying a word about God, that we are fallible, but savable. We, as humans, even though we may not have ill intent, sometimes make the wrong call. But that doesn't mean that we cannot be redeemed through the actions we take following the fall.

I swear, I will never forget the pain I felt as I confessed my sin to my dad. Nor will I forget that he did not, even for a moment, judge me for my mistake, but merely steered me to the right path from that point forward.

Isn't that what our Lord does for us every day?

Buried Burdens

Ms. Joan

I am a child of God. I was raised Catholic with high morals and a healthy lifestyle. Yet, I make mistakes, fall short and feel shame. I have lost my temper with loved ones. I have held positions and lost jobs suddenly. I have hurt people's feelings and been afraid to apologize and restore those relationships. I am human; I try, I fail, I hold onto all those hurts, and I recycle them.

Today, while listening to day forty-two of the "Bible in a Year" podcast with Father Mike Schmitz, God spoke to me.

This is what I was led to understand: We are given God's laws and commandments to follow and to honor Him. When we disobey, we are encouraged to confess our sins, ask for forgiveness, change our behavior and return to God's love and grace.

I paused, brought to mind some long-buried burdens, and offered them up. As I shed some tears, I felt an overwhelming sense of our Heavenly Father's peace and tranquility envelop me.

"So, you also are now in anguish. But I will see you again, and your hearts will rejoice, and no one will take your joy away from you." John 16:22

"I Love You"

M. A. B.

One morning I woke up before my family, and I was sitting on the couch praying. In my prayer I asked God, "What do you want me to know?" I heard a voice in my head say, "That I love you." I often have trouble being sure whether a "voice" is from God, or just my imagination, but not this time. I'm positive it was from Him.

"...and that Christ may dwell in your hearts through faith; that you, rooted and grounded in love, may have strength to comprehend with all the holy ones what is the breadth and length and height and depth, and to know the love of Christ that surpasses knowledge, so that you may be filled with all the fullness of God." Ephesians 3:17-19

A Thorn Tree

Claire Patterson

During our trip to Medjugorje[11] in July 2001, I was climbing Apparition Hill[2] alone and saying my rosary. As pilgrims follow the path up the hill, there are images displayed of each mystery to aid the pilgrim in meditation. As I reached the third sorrowful mystery, the crowning of thorns, I saw that my shadow was falling on the bas-relief and it was difficult to see the carving of Christ and the Roman soldiers.

I decided to back up until my shadow moved away from the image, so that the sunlight could illuminate the scene. I bent over slightly while walking and focused my eyes on the ground, so as not to trip over the large rocks and uneven footing. When my shadow moved far enough away, I stopped and stood erect.

Immediately my head was pierced by thorns. I cried, "Ouch!" and jerked forward to escape the pain. Turning around, I discovered that I had backed into a large thorn tree!

Then I began a serious meditation on the sufferings of our Blessed Lord. Jesus could not move away to avoid the thorns piercing his head as I had done. The cruel Romans were holding him in place as they pounded the instrument of torture onto his head.

Lord, never let me forget your suffering for my redemption.

"...Give Thanks to the Lord, acclaim His name;
among the nations make known His deeds, proclaim
how exalted is His Name." Isaiah 12:4

The Spiritual and Corporal Works of Mercy

Janet H.

At Sunday Mass some years ago, the priest made mention in his homily of the Spiritual and Corporal Works of Mercy[30]. As he spoke, I realized that I could not remember all of the Works of Mercy in each list. When we got home from Mass, I went straight to the bookcase to find the complete lists of the Spiritual and Corporal Works of Mercy.

As I was searching, my husband called from the other room, "What's for lunch?"

It was winter, and I usually fixed a hot lunch after Sunday Mass. Since lunch had now become the priority, I asked the Lord to help me find the lists because I had to stop my search and get lunch ready. My husband was hungry! After lunch I forgot all about resuming my search.

It was a couple of nights later that I woke up in the middle of the night. The house was quiet and my husband was sleeping. I was wide awake and there was no going back to sleep.

So, I went downstairs to the kitchen and put the tea kettle on the stove. I made the tea and went into the other room, sat down, and turned on the TV, which was already tuned to the EWTN station.

Immediately I heard, "Good evening, I am Fr. Trigilio and I would like to speak to you tonight about the Spiritual and Corporal Works of Mercy." I almost dropped my teacup because I was laughing so hard! (I know the Lord was laughing with me.) In the midst of my laughter, I said out loud, "Lord, you are so funny! Look what you just did!" I had asked Him to help me find those lists, and He did!

After the show was over, and I had both lists of the Works of Mercy, I reflected on what had just happened. God knew exactly how much time I would lie awake in bed before coming downstairs and exactly how much time I would be in the kitchen making tea. So, He knew exactly what time to wake me up, so that I would be sitting in front of the TV to hear Fr. Trigilio's words.

I reflected on how God is always with us; not only in our big, important decisions and trials in our lives, but also in our daily, ordinary, smallest, seemingly trivial, moments of our lives.

God is good all the time.

"I'm Not You"

Anonymous

I was born and baptized into a Catholic family. I've received all the relevant Sacraments. I married in the Catholic Church and sent my kids to Catholic School. Check, check, check and check.

I grew up a tomboy-ish country bumpkin of modest means. I loved to read; I worked hard and did well in school. I got my first job at a diner at age sixteen, and when my parents divorced three years later, I was forced into financial independence. I dropped out of college after receiving an Associate's Degree, and stepped up to full-time employment.

I landed a job with a prestigious global brand strategy firm, and had the opportunity to travel around the world. Outwardly, I was strong, capable, determined and confident. (I had to be, to survive.) Inwardly, I was insecure, envious and fearful. I was an imposter, hobnobbing with worldly, sophisticated MBA's. But I checked all the right boxes to get through. My head and heart were hard as nails; my eyes were focused on my career and family. There was little time for God; I was too BUSY.

My husband and I had two sons who went to Catholic schools, where they received a solid education and the religious training we felt unqualified to provide at home. School was never easy for my oldest son, and it was difficult for me to understand him. I was the independent, overachieving jetsetter, and I couldn't comprehend why he didn't ace every task. We fought continually. My survival mantra was, "strong, capable, accomplished!" My son did not share my perspective. He was a free spirit and I was a super-mom control freak.

At his pre-school graduation he didn't want to wear the shirt I had laid out for him. I got so angry I flung it at him. It flicked his face and left a mark on his cheek that was visible during the ceremony. I didn't receive the "mother of the year" trophy for that year!

He was bullied in grade school, but wouldn't stand up for himself. He barely passed the high school entrance exam. He was outgoing and funny with his friends, but quiet and moody at home.

I once confided my frustration with him to an acquaintance who advised me to have a "meditative conversation" with him. I did, and asked him why he would not take his studies more seriously. Why he was not driven to succeed? Why did he continue to fall short of my expectations? His answer was simple: "I'm not you." I realize now, that it wasn't my son speaking to me. It had been God with the ruthless clarity I needed to hear.

It rocked me to the core. I realized how controlling I had been, and how I projected my stress onto him. From that moment forward, I embrace him for exactly who he is. I focus on his strengths and on my shortcomings. A crack appeared in my hardened heart. I started listening instead of talking. I listen better now to my children, my family, my friends, my colleagues, and a little bit more to God.

My son managed to graduate from high school and get into college, where he found himself on academic suspension after the first year. I was disappointed and sad for him, but this time, there was no anger or shame. He sat out a semester and enrolled in the community college where he dropped classes (unbeknownst to me) and continued to struggle.

He loved living with his buds at college, but my husband and I decided it was not prudent to continue to fund his college "education." So, I had a hard conversation with him, and he decided to take another break from school and find a job. During that time, he would decide his next steps.

He learned of a potential part-time opportunity at a transportation company and was called in for an interview. Now, I'm pretty sure this is not a Catholic-sanctioned tactic, but at that time I "made a deal with God." I promised God that if my son got the job, I would start going to church every Sunday. I knew that this job could provide him the opportunity to continue with a good, reputable company, if he chose not to return to college. Well, praise God, he got the job, and I held true to my promise; I attended Mass every week.

One Sunday after Mass, two women from the parish, who knew me through our children's sports events, eagerly invited me to an upcoming Christ Renews His Parish (CRHP)[4] retreat. I didn't even know what CRHP was, and politely said, "I'll think about it." I really didn't take the invitation seriously. After all, these women were pillars of our parish, while I hadn't been to Mass regularly for many years. But, it kept nagging at me. I felt called to go, but also felt intimidated by my uncultivated spiritual development. I was afraid I'd be judged, and would feel like an outsider, and would be embarrassed by my religious immaturity. Still, I felt a calling.

If you've ever traveled by air, you've heard the flight attendant make this statement as part of her safety announcement: "If the cabin pressure changes, masks will fall from the compartment above your seat. If this happens secure your own mask first before assisting others and continue to breathe normally."

Think about this statement. The implication is that you will be in a better position to assist someone else if you first take the time to attend to yourself.

I realized that I needed to overcome my insecurities and help myself, so I signed up for the weekend, thanks to the initial nudge from my two friends, and God's continued nudge. I entered the retreat with all my apprehensions, insecurities and fears; I left a changed woman - full of the love of Christ. I had finally answered His call with wide open eyes, ears, and heart. I had never experienced such amazing love, courage, wisdom, vulnerability and spirituality as I did on that weekend. I learned that we are not put on this earth to go through the motions and check boxes. We must celebrate the life God has given us, use His gifts, listen to His Word, and courageously share His love with others. I also realized that none of us can do it alone.

Since that first CRHP retreat, I've led one weekend retreat and participated in others at our parish. I also participated in a Cursillo[5] weekend. I am in a weekly prayer group, "Walking with Purpose,"[29] a women's parish group and a Catholic book club. I've read the Bible twice and am currently reading the Catechism. I drove five hundred seventy-five miles to see the Pope. I attend Mass every Sunday, and sometimes during the week as well. I visit Jesus in Adoration[1] once a week.

I have a special prayer area in my home, and I'm surrounded by amazing friends, priests and nuns who inspire me to not just stay on course, but to continue to grow in my faith. I'm finished being an imposter. I embrace the gifts God has given to me, and work each and every day to build a closer relationship with Him through service and study. I still consider myself a spiritual novice, because there is so much more to learn and grasp and embrace, but I am committed for the rest of my life. There is nothing else in my life that compares to the joy and exaltation of my commitment to Christ.

And what happened with our son? As you know by now, he's no literary genius or rocket scientist. But I don't care that he didn't get a college degree or that he probably doesn't make as much money as many of his friends. (They don't care either.) I am so proud of the man he's become. He has a good job, a nice home, a wicked sense of humor, great friends and most importantly, a kind heart. We've never talked about how my hardened heart may have influenced his development, but we might someday. I pray every day that he opens his heart to the grace of God in order to come to know Him, love Him and serve Him as I endeavor to do now.

Below is an excerpt from his letter given to me during my CRHP retreat. Hopefully it makes you laugh as much as I did:

> "Mom,
>
> What can be said about you that hasn't already been said about Mother Teresa? Ha -ha. I'm just kidding, but not really. I may not be the best person in the world but when I am a better person, it is because of you; you

> inspire me to be a better person and I love you very much. I will keep you in my prayers."

Another God moment? Yes, because to me, it's proof that the Lord is truly with and in every one of us, and that it is through Him that all good things come. I wasted a lot of years going through the motions – just checking boxes – but my eyes, ears and heart are wide open now.

"Thanks be to God for His indescribable gift!" 2 Corinthians 9:15

"Keep me safe, O God; In You I take refuge. I say to the Lord, 'You are my Lord. You are my only good.'" Psalm 16:1-2

An Act of Forgiveness

Pat Hunt

Ever since I was a small child I was interested in genealogy. I felt like it was an undiscovered part of me waiting to be explored. I became even more fascinated when a wealth of information became available on the Internet.

Around 2002 I visited a lady I knew casually, who lived a few miles away. She was selling genealogy books and, of course, I was interested. We chatted about our backgrounds to find areas in which we may have a common ancestry. Somehow, Estill County, Kentucky came up during our conversation.

I told her about a story that I discovered by doing research involving my great-great-great grandfather, Thomas Canter. I learned that in 1825 he and his brother-in-law, Joel Martin, were involved in stealing a beehive full of honey. This beehive was valued at five dollars at that time. Evidently, a feud ensued between the Canter and Martin families, mostly involving the brothers of Joel.

This lady astounded me by saying that she was related to the same Martin family. She printed out numerous pages of information on that family. How is it possible that two people, practically strangers, get together one hundred and seventy-five years later to discuss a feud that happened in an obscure area of Kentucky?

I am a Catholic and she is not. I immediately said, "All is forgiven in the spirit world between the Canters and the Martins!" It was a special moment. We laughed and experienced a great camaraderie over this incident. It was like an act of forgiveness after so many years of feuding. I felt like souls could be forgiven!

Her family was amazed by the coincidence and started calling me the "Beehive Lady".

I could see God's hand in possibly releasing some souls from Purgatory. Of course, there is no proof, but it certainly felt inspired! The experience made me feel like the hand of God was definitely there!

What's in Your Cup?

Barbara C. DeNamur

The Holy Spirit gave me a lesson to share with the "Ladies of Lunch and Prayer." We meet twice a month to say the rosary and eat lunch together. This lesson has become known as "What's in Your Cup?"

If you have a cup of coffee, and someone bumps into you, and the coffee spills, why did coffee spill from your cup? Many people try to answer this question with phrases like, "Because someone bumped your arm." or "Your cup was too full." The true answer is because coffee was in your cup! It seems too simple. However, if tea or juice were in the cup, <u>that</u> would have spilled out, not coffee. There are times when life jostles us or turns our day upside down. What will spill out of us? It is worth a thought and maybe a change in behavior.

After I got this idea, I had a nudge from the Holy Spirit to write a poem about this concept. It was difficult to begin writing this poem. Nothing I wrote sounded quite right and a lot of scrap paper went into the recycle bin.

That week I was asked to pray for an hour before the Blessed Sacrament, during Eucharistic Adoration[1], to fill in for a designated adorer. I took a pencil and paper with me. As I sat in silence in the nearly empty church and stared at the monstrance with the Sacred Body of Jesus, I asked the Holy Spirit to assist me in this task. The words came to me in waves. They came so fast I could hardly write them down. After an hour, I had a rough draft, but it wasn't finished.

Working on the poem by myself produced nothing of worth. The next week, I was back at Eucharistic Adoration asking for help from the Holy Spirit. More words came into my mind and corrections came easily. The poem was better, but not polished.

That night, right before I fell asleep, the message came to me that I needed a Bible verse in the poem. This seemed like a daunting task that I planned to tackle in the morning. As I read the Bible the next day, I was led to James 1:19-20. This verse was perfect for the poem and for the concept of "What's in Your Cup?"

What's in Your Cup?

Did someone jostle your arm
As they were passing you by?
Oops, there goes your favorite cup.
Its contents begin to fly!

Why did you spill your coffee
Onto the clean tile floor?
Because coffee filled your cup.
Ponder this a little more.

Say, you had a cup of tea
Or chocolate milk or some juice.
Whatever fills your cup
Will spill. It's the honest truth.

When life comes by and shakes you,
Whatever's inside will spill out.
Life gets tough. It will happen.
Would you curse or swear or shout?

Ask yourself, "What's in my cup?"
You know the "you" deep inside.
Is there humble peace and love?
Or does bitter hate abide?

Always be quick to listen,
Slow to speak and slow to wrath.
Humbly accepting God's Word
As He shows you the right path.

It is God who gives you life
And creates for you the cup.
You are the one to decide
Just how you fill it up.

B. DeNamur

"Know this, my dear brothers: everyone should be quick to hear, slow to speak, slow to wrath, for the wrath of a man does not accomplish the righteousness of God." James 1:19-20

St. Anthony

Anonymous

In December 2022, I was working with the OCIA[16] Catechumen group from our Parish. I was sharing my book on The Holy Souls in Purgatory with them. The book marker I was using contained a relic of St. Anthony. I noticed that one of the Catechumen candidates was using his missal, but he didn't have a book marker for it. On impulse, I gave him mine.

After our session, this man shared with me that when he had lost his grandfather's pocketknife, he began praying to St. Anthony to find it. He made a deal with God, and St. Anthony, that if he found the pocketknife, he would become a Catholic. He recovered the knife soon after his promise, and not long after that, he signed up for the OCIA classes. He also chose St. Anthony as his confirmation saint. He was confirmed at the Easter Vigil Mass in 2023! Praise God!

I did not recognize it at the time, but the relic of St. Anthony was very meaningful for this wonderful young man, and that "impulse" was God speaking to my heart.

PART II

Saved by the Angels

*"For God commands the angels to guard you in all your ways.
With their hands they shall support you, lest
you strike your foot against a stone"*
Psalm 91:11-12

CHAPTER 6

Angels to Help

"Tobiah went to look for someone acquainted with the roads who would travel with him to Media. As soon as he went out, he found the angel Raphael standing before him, though he did not know that this was an angel of God." Tobit 5:4

Walking with an Angel on 42nd Street in New York City

Barbara C. DeNamur

I was awe-struck as I walked down 42nd Street in the fall of 1965. This was my first trip out of Michigan. My eyes were a bit blurry with lack of sleep as I left Grand Central Station. The trip to New York was planned by my Uncle Jim as a high school graduation gift. There was a bit of a chill in the early morning air, so I wore a cardigan sweater and my best white gloves. The sidewalk was way wider than the sidewalks in the Village of Holly, Michigan where I had grown-up. The buildings were so tall that I had to crane my neck to see them, as the early morning sun peaked around each one. I was swinging my brand-new white Samsonite luggage, a high school graduation gift, and greeting passers-by with, "Hello" and, "Nice morning." Most of them ignored me or made a funny face. This seemed like a dream to wake up in a strange bustling city.

The directions my uncle had sent to me were somewhere in my purse. As I read the directions, I was supposed to take West 42nd Street. Why did he have to say west and not right or left? There were yellow and black checkered cabs everywhere, but I could not afford to take a taxi.

I stood still for a few moments trying to get my bearings and said a little prayer that God would help me find my way. When I looked up, there was a young man running in my direction. He stopped in front of me, catching his breath, and asked if I had just left the train from Detroit. "I am one of the engineers who work on passenger trains for the C&O Railroad. Name's Augustine, but the guys who work on the train just call me Gus." Gus was dressed in a light blue polo shirt and jeans, but he wore sturdy work shoes that were scuffed. My curiosity peaked; was he telling me the truth?

"I saw you sleeping on the train as I made my rounds last night. You used your sweater for a pillow, trying to get comfortable in your seat. I thought you might need some help. Would you like me to help you?"

To sleep, I <u>had</u> wrapped my sweater around my purse to form a pillow.

At that moment, I felt vulnerable for the first time since I left the train. My wide-eyed wonder of this adventure came to a screeching halt.

Feeling the need to let him know that I was cared for by some important people, I started explaining. "My Uncle Jim is a professor at Columbia University and is teaching classes, so he could not greet me at the train depot. He and Aunt Dotty live in Tenafly, N. J. My uncle has a PHD in Chemical Engineering and has applied for several patents. He wanted me to take the subway, but I am afraid to go below ground. Now I need to find the Port Authority Bus Terminal."

Gus smiled, "Yes, I have been there many times. I know the place well and can show you how to get there. Would you like me to carry your baggage?" I handed him my suitcase and kept my train case, which was packed with personal items. We walked in silence as my mind went crazy with thoughts of "What am I doing? Can I trust this man? I need his help, so please Lord, keep me safe."

Gus broke the silence with, "Are you hungry?" "Yes," I answered, "But I don't have much money, and I need to buy my ticket to Tenafly." Gus looked at me with kind eyes and said, "I know a small diner up the street where you can get an egg, a piece of toast and a cup of coffee for two dollars. Come on, I'll show you." We walked along briskly and came to a small diner. A big sign on the door read, "Best and Cheapest Breakfast in N.Y. - $2."

We went in and sat at the counter to eat our breakfast. I can't remember what we talked about. I probably told him I was going to start college in a week and study to be an elementary school teacher.

After breakfast, we walked down to Broadway as Gus pointed out different buildings and landmarks. We took a left and then a right onto 41st Street and walked to 8th Avenue and the Port Authority Bus Terminal. Gus told me there were different ticket windows and to look for the city name, Tenafly. "Get in that line and you will be all set. I hope you have an enjoyable stay with your uncle. I know you will have fun at the World's Fair."

We walked into this echoing rotund building that was bustling with people. My eyes were glued to the different ticket window signs. I found the window I needed and got in line. When I turned around to thank Gus for all his help, he was gone. I looked into the crowd but could not find him. He had just vanished. I thought that it was a bit strange, but the whole episode was strange. I said a quiet prayer thanking God for keeping me safe and bought my ticket.

This story was never shared with my family for fear that they would not trust me to travel on my own again. The memory lay dormant until many years later. I was reading the story of Tobit in the Bible, Chapter 5:4-6. Tobiah, Tobit's son, was looking for someone to help him travel to Media. He sees Raphael, the angel, standing there, though he doesn't know he is an angel. Tobiah asks Raphael, Do you know the way to Media?" "Yes," he replied, "I have been there many times. I know the place well and am acquainted with all the routes."

This made me wonder, "Did God send the Archangel Raphael to help me find my way? Or was Gus simply a Good Samaritan?"

"I can now tell you that when you, Tobit, and Sarah prayed, it was I who presented and read the record of your prayer before the Glory of the Lord....I am Raphael, one of the seven angels who enter and serve before the Glory of the Lord." Tobit 12:12-15

"Angel of God, My Guardian Dear"

A. T.

In mid-December I was at a church in northern Kentucky as an employee for a funeral home. I had arrived early to prepare for the services.

As I was preparing for the funeral, I noticed a woman collecting wrapped presents that had been donated for the church's giving tree. As there were many packages, I offered to help her take them out of the church and into her van.

Since it was cold outside, I was moving very quickly, and I tripped over the curb as I was heading back into church. I started falling forward and was about to hit the ground, but suddenly I was upright again. The woman asked me if I was OK, and I said, "I'm fine, but I can't believe I didn't fall!" She said, "Your Guardian Angel was looking out for you." I know this was true because there was no other explanation why I didn't crash my face into the cement walk-way.

I thanked God and my Guardian Angel for saving me from injury.

"Angel of God, my Guardian dear, to whom God's
love commits me here. Ever this day be at my side,
to light and guard, to rule and guide."

Angel with a Tire Iron

Claire Patterson

On January 30, 1974, my husband, Duke, and I were driving to San Juan, Puerto Rico, for our flight home to Cincinnati. We had been living on Ramey Air Force base near Aguadilla since July 1973, and had shipped most of our belongings back to the U.S. via the Navy's transfer system.

Around midnight we got a flat tire a few miles outside of San Juan. It was raining hard. We pulled over, not sure what to do next. We had a tight schedule to keep.

Before long, a car pulled ahead of us, stopped, and a man got out. He asked Duke if he could help. Duke was standing in the rain with the trunk of our car open, and the tire iron in his hand. The man took the tire iron from him and began taking the flat off of the car, while Duke held the spare.

I was concerned that the stranger might hit Duke over the head with the tire iron, and steal anything we had worth taking. I began to look around for a place to run for help.

Surprisingly, the tire was changed quickly, the man gave Duke the tire iron back and got into his car and took off. We looked at each other and said, "That must have been an angel sent from God." There was no other logical explanation!

We were able to drive our car to the Naval Base in San Juan for transport to North Carolina, and then ride the bus to the airport in time to catch our flight to Cincinnati. Thanks be to God!

Encounter With an Angel

Anonymous

As I was going through a divorce, I decided to attend a weekend retreat for divorced, separated, and widowed people. Their brochure mentioned "forgiveness," which was something I was looking for.

The retreat was in Dayton, Ohio at a time before the invention of GPS systems, so I was following a paper map to get to the retreat center. Unfortunately, I got lost and ended up on a dirt road somewhere in Dayton. Frustrated, I put my map down on the passenger seat and put my head on the steering wheel, trying to decide if I should just find my way home.

Suddenly, a white pick-up truck pulled up next to me, and the driver rolled down his window and asked if I needed help. I told him I was going to the Bergamo Retreat Center, but was lost. He told me to go down the next road, turn left, then right into the parking lot. I thanked him, looked down at the map next to me, looked back up, and there was no white truck, no driver, and not even dust coming off the road. It seemed I had encountered an angel to guide me.

I made it to the retreat center on time, completed the weekend, and was able to write a letter of forgiveness to my ex-wife. Later that next week, I received a call to be a team member on the next weekend to help others with their journey of forgiveness. Ten years later, I was still on the team, fully recovered and married to my present wife and former team member.

The encounter with the angel started me on my path to peace and ministry for the rest of my life.

Angels on the Highway

Claire Patterson

In February, 1976, Duke and I were driving home to Norfolk, Virginia, after visiting family in Cincinnati. We were making the trip in one drive, as we did not have enough money for a hotel. It was approaching 2:00 a.m., and we were navigating along a twisting, two-lane road in the mountains of Tennessee.

Duke was at the wheel, and I was sleeping in the front seat. Christopher, our six-week-old baby, was sleeping in his infant seat behind us. Suddenly we were face down in a ditch at about a forty-five-degree angle. Chris had been thrown out of his seat. He was screaming, but was unhurt.

As I comforted my baby, we looked in our wallets to see if we could afford a tow, if (and that was a big IF) we could get a tow. We only had enough money for gas to get home.

Suddenly, two cars stopped on the road above us. Eight strong-looking men got out and began climbing down the hill toward us. They offered to help. I strapped Chris into his seat, got behind the wheel to steer, and Duke and the young men pushed the car up the hill and back onto the road.

We had sustained no damage to the car nor to ourselves. Duke took out his wallet to give the guys his last twenty dollars, and they were suddenly gone. We got home safely, praising God for His protection, and for sending His angels to help.

"See, I am sending an angel before you, to guard you on the way and bring you to the place I have prepared." Exodus 23:20

Wing-Tipped Shoes

Suzanne Millay

I was sitting alone in church and feeling particularly low one day.

As I was praying, I heard a voice in my head say, "What kind of shoes do angels wear?" There was a pause, and then I heard the answer, "Wing-tipped!"

I couldn't help but laugh out loud. Apparently, my Guardian Angel has a sense of humor.

Looking up at the altar, I gazed at the choirs of angels painted on the wall.

They do indeed have on wing-tipped shoes!

CHAPTER 7

Angels to Save

Hanging by a Diaper

R. K.

It was the summer of 1980 and I had been married for eight years. We had two little boys; the older boy was not quite four, and the younger one was a sixteen-month-old toddler.

We decided to buy our first house that year. It was an older, beautiful two-story house. The upstairs bedrooms were spacious with large closets. The closets had no doors which turned out to be perfect. We set up a play area in the boys' room with print animals on the walls. They loved it and playing inside the closet was like having their own camp. In our master bedroom, there was an oversized access door that led to the roof over our porch. This door was kept locked and was very difficult to open.

There were a lot of kids in the neighborhood. One day, four children came over to play upstairs with my boys. There were two six-year-olds and two four-year-olds, in addition to my two children. When I checked on them, they were all having a good time. I told them to be sure to stay in the boys' bedroom.

I went down to the kitchen to prepare for dinner. I picked up a potato and the peeler and made only one swipe. Without thinking, I dropped them into the sink and hurried right back upstairs.

At the top of the stairs, I saw that the access door to the roof was open, and I could see all of the kids on the roof, except my toddler, Michael. As I climbed outside onto the roof, I saw Kathy, the six-year-old girl, holding on to his cloth diaper to keep Michael from falling off the roof! I rushed over and lifted him back up to safety. When I examined him, I found a rash on his belly from the roof tile, but otherwise, he was fine.

I was quite shaken, but realized that it had been Divine intervention for both Kathy and me to spring into action that quickly, saving my child's life.

I still get chills and say a prayer of thanks when that incident comes to mind. I have been grateful my whole life to Kathy and for my heavenly inspiration. I have always felt that it was Michael's guardian angel who nudged both of us to act swiftly. I have been truly grateful ever since.

I still don't know how those kids got that door open, but having learned from that incident, we moved our bed in front of that door!!!

Thank you, God, for saving my child.

"It's Not Your Time to Die."

Claire Patterson

When Duke, my husband, was twelve years old, he was terribly sick and in the hospital with an infection and a high fever. His mother feared for his life. At one point, Duke saw an angel in his room who told him not to worry, declaring, "It's not your time to die."

The Fear of Death

Pam Ryan-Rettig

In mid-November of 2021, I was not feeling well. I went to the doctor, thinking I had a sinus infection. I assumed my appointment would end with the doctor prescribing an antibiotic. I was wrong. The doctor wasn't sure it was bacterial. Within a couple of days, I started feeling worse.

The national conversation about COVID was always changing. My boyfriend, Bill, thirty-five miles away, bought some COVID tests and came to visit with me for a while. I was so grateful he did, because I tested positive for the disease.

He did some research and learned about a treatment that mitigated the severity of a COVID infection and shortened the recovery time. The medicine was called monoclonal antibody infusion, but it had to be administered within seven days of the onset of the disease.

Bless his big heart, he found out that a COVID test from Walgreens did not qualify for medical coverage. So, the next day he drove me to Covington where a huge field was devoted to outdoor testing. We ended up in a long winding line of hundreds of cars until we arrived at the testing tent hours later.

The COVID testers promised they would email my test result after midnight that same night.

The seven-day clock was counting down. We finally received an official positive result the next morning. My kind boyfriend called for an appointment with St. Elizabeth Hospital for two shots in each arm of the monoclonal infusion. They administered the four shots on Wednesday, November 17th, and then sent me home.

Bill was my hero. After we arrived back at my condo, he stayed with me and noticed I was sleeping a lot; I was really "out of it." Thank goodness he felt he should purchase an oximeter, a device for reading pulse rate and blood oxygen level.

The oximeter showed my oxygen dropping to critical levels. At 3:00 a.m. he called 911. Had he not been there to make the call, I would have died in my sleep.

When I woke up in the emergency room on Friday morning, I was so frightened. Bill was not allowed to be with me. Since the hospital did not have any vacant COVID rooms, I did not get assigned a room until 4:00 p.m. the next day.

It was touch and go for me for over two days. As I laid there praying and praying, I imagined the angels were surrounding my bed. They had protected me ever since I was a little girl, but I thought this might be my time to leave the Earth. I can't keep tears out of my eyes as I write this story. I was starting to wonder if I would live to see my grandkids ever again.

The doctors and nurses were so kind to me. During my nine-day stay in the hospital, I was allowed to have one visitor each day for one hour. Bill would visit me with a gown, mask, and surgical cap. I did not want my daughter to visit, because I was fearful of infecting her, her husband and their children. I hoped to watch daily Mass on TV and receive Communion each day. Neither were available. However, Bill would bring Jesus to me by reading the Gospel from each daily Mass.

I prayed and prayed during this time, and I am still thanking Bill, our Blessed Mother, the Holy Trinity, and the angels for helping me make it through that scary journey. I wrote the doctors and staff a long, heartfelt letter of thanks for their outstanding care! I have much to be thankful for!

"But the Lord's messenger called to him from heaven, 'Abraham, Abraham!' 'Yes, Lord,' he answered. 'Do not lay your hand on the boy,' said the messenger. 'Do not do the least thing to him. I know how devoted you are to God, since you did not withhold from me your own beloved son.'" Genesis 22:11-12

9/11

Claire Patterson

So many stories of 9/11 are sad, but this perspective has always lifted my spirits.

It was the account that involved all of the people who should have been in the Twin Towers, the Pentagon, or on the plane that crashed in Pennsylvania; but were not.

At the time of the attack, people who were customarily on time for things, for unexplainable reasons, were not where they should have been.

I like to imagine their Guardian Angels being very busy that morning: hiding car keys, blocking taxis, unplugging alarm clocks, etc., to keep those in their care from harm.

My Guardian Angel at Work

Clare Rodgers

We were sitting at a recently installed stoplight, behind another car. I had just picked up my daughter, Elizabeth, and her friend, Colleen, from kindergarten. They were sitting in the backseat with my four-year-old son, Louis, talking and laughing.

As was typical of my efficient self, I was taking advantage of the moment by straightening some items on the car's console. A piece of paper fluttered to the floor of the car, so I reached down to pick it up. When I looked up, the stoplight had changed to green, and the car in front of me had successfully turned left onto the intersecting road. I was silently berating myself for taking my eye off the light and holding up the cars behind me. I released my foot from the brake and began to go forward, when a car from the intersecting road sped past me, running a red light. I quickly applied the brake again.

The children and I became very still. Even the driver behind me had a look of shock on her face as we all realized that we had narrowly missed being struck broadside by the speeding car.

Our guardian angels, sent from God, were certainly busy that day caring for His children!

We Didn't Hit a Single Tree

Claire Patterson

It was the winter of 2000. I was driving my son, Chris, to his job on a snowy evening. We were out in the middle of nowhere, on a twisting two-lane road in Northern Kentucky. It was dark, and I was driving slowly. Chris said, "You know, Mom, the speed limit here is forty-miles per-hour."

So, to make him happy, I began to speed up. Immediately, I hit a patch of ice and my car started spinning out of control. Chris leaned over and wrapped his arms around me, in an attempt to shield me from harm, as we skidded off the road and down a steep hill covered with trees.

Unbelievably, we reached the bottom of the hill without hitting a single tree. We both jumped out of the car unhurt. There was no cell service in our area, so Chris climbed up the hill and walked about a quarter of a mile to the nearest house to call for a tow truck. As I waited for him, I walked up the hill following the car tracks. It occurred to me that we should have hit at least two trees on the way down, but we didn't.

The tow truck was able to pull my car to the top of the hill and back onto the road. I drove about twenty miles per hour the rest of the way to Chris' place of employment, and all the way home. My car was not damaged, from what I could see.

The next day I took my car to a service shop to have them check the undercarriage for any necessary repairs. They found a collection of mud and grass underneath my car, and when they washed it off, I was good to go.

I am sure our Guardian Angels guided us safely down that hill.

"Suddenly, the angel of the Lord stood by him and a light shone in the cell. He tapped Peter on the side and awakened him saying, 'Get up quickly.' The chains fell from his wrists....Then Peter recovered his senses and said, 'Now I know for certain that the Lord sent his angel and rescued me from the hand of Herod and from all that the Jewish people had been expecting.'"
Acts 12:7-11

"St. Michael, Defend Us!"

Peggy B.

I was driving home to visit my parents. It was three hundred and fifteen miles from my doorstep to theirs. I had driven this route so often over the years that my car's GPS automatically knew the backroads I should take to avoid traffic. It has been my habit to pray the rosary, while driving. I keep my rosary handy on my rearview mirror for these journeys.

I was on Rt. 65 heading toward the Chicago area, when an extension ladder flew off of a pickup truck that was ahead in the lane next to me. As I watched the ladder skid on the highway, I could see that it was headed straight for my lane and my car. It was one of those instances where you think, "Should I brake, slow down, pull over... or what?"

As I called out St. Michael's name, the extension ladder was in front of me, and then just as quickly slid over to the shoulder of the highway.

"St. Michael the Archangel, defend us in battle!" Indeed, he does!

Falling in Slow Motion

Amy Hartig

In 1994, we lived in an old farmhouse with a trap door to our basement. One day I descended to the basement to check the wood stove. I asked my older daughters to keep my two-year-old toddler out of the hallway and thus, away from the open trap door.

Just as I was about to climb back upstairs, I heard someone scream. As I looked up, the baby was falling through the opening. I couldn't move as I looked on in fear. She fell in what appeared to be slow motion. It was like an Angel caught her and gently laid her down. I thought perhaps my grandma, who had recently died, might have been praying for us as well.

I feared that my daughter had broken her neck from the height of the fall. She was bleeding and crying, but moving. We rushed her to the hospital only to find out she had a chipped tooth and a minor abrasion.

I could only attribute this to God's intervention, as my baby should have been seriously injured.

This same daughter has experienced, later in life, a couple of car accidents from which she escaped serious injuries. I believe her Guardian Angel is watching over her all the time!

"See that you do not despise one of these little ones, for I say to you, that their angels in heaven always look upon the face of My heavenly Father." Matthew 18:10

Guardian Angel Takes the Wheel

Joe Gering

In 1982 I was driving on Highway 74 to a business appointment. I was very tired and fell asleep at the wheel. When I woke up, I found myself parked in a truck weigh station with the engine still running. I was refreshed from my "nap" and wondering how I had gotten there. I said a quick prayer of thanksgiving and finished my trip.

The Rastafarian Angel

Christopher Patterson

This is a story about a covenant I made with God, how and why I broke that agreement, and how I felt afterward. This is also about how my contrition and petition for mercy opened the floodgates of God's grace to come pouring in.

It began with a pilgrimage. Yes, a religious pilgrimage, but, I was seeking inspiration about a theological matter far different from that of most pilgrims. You see, I was at a place in my life where I was transitioning from Hare Krishna to Christianity. Even though I had been baptized in the Catholic faith, I had drifted away from the Church during my college years. So, I decided to travel to Venezuela where I might visit with Maria Esperanza (1928-2004). She was known as a mystic, and it was reported that she had been experiencing apparitions of the Blessed Virgin Mary.

I wanted to immerse myself at the site of Maria's apparitions and let the Holy Spirit guide me, because there was still a part of me that was holding on to the Hare Krishna faith. Even though I was not able to meet with the visionary, the trip was beneficial to me in so many ways. I feel I touched many souls. I felt the Holy Spirit guiding my footsteps throughout this pilgrimage. Some of these experiences were:

- While I was waiting for a bus at 2:00 a.m., I ran into someone who really needed to hear the Gospel. I approached him unafraid, and as we spoke, he began to feel more at peace and strengthened by God's love.
- I met many families who encouraged my faith. I learned how important family is, and I felt like a part of theirs while enjoying their hospitality. I think that during those times, I really helped a lot of people, and they helped me.

Returning home from the pilgrimage in Venezuela, I inadvertently departed the plane in Kingston, Jamaica, instead of the second airport on that island. My checked bag was on its way to Cincinnati, but I had missed my flight to Atlanta.

After I realized my mistake, I looked in my pockets and backpack. I had only $5.00 to my name. I looked around the airport for a bank, and couldn't find one. Since I couldn't afford a taxi, I decided to walk from the airport to central Kingston. I really needed to find a bank where I could call my mom to have her wire enough money to me to buy a plane ticket to get home. If there was a bank in the airport, I had missed it.

I was very naïve, because I didn't understand the danger into which I was walking.

I'll never forget the look a police officer gave me as he passed in his vehicle on the way to the airport. His gaze said, "What are you doing?" That made me a little nervous, but I kept walking because I didn't have an alternative. As I continued to walk toward Kingston, another police officer drove by. His eyes said, "Are you stupid? Are you trying to get yourself killed?"

I became more and more anxious about my plan to go into the city.

As I was walking along the highway, I began thinking that I was being punished by God because I had eaten meat on the plane traveling from Venezuela. I had been very hungry when I boarded the plane, because I had not eaten for a while, and all they offered me was a sausage. I had been nearly broke for several days before my journey home, and ate very little, causing me to lose a few pounds that I didn't need to lose. I was practically starving, so I ate meat, for the first time in over a year, on that plane.

I had become a vegetarian for religious reasons, so I believed I had broken my covenant with God. As I walked along the road, I began praying that God would have mercy on me and send an angel to protect me. Something within me strongly affirmed that my prayer would be answered.

Suddenly a car pulled over. The driver, a young dark-skinned Rastafarian with long dread locks said, "What are you doing?" I said, "I'm trying to walk to town to get some money wired to me, because I missed my flight." He said, "Mon, just hop in because you don't want to go around the next corner. It's not good for you to walk any further. Get in the car. I'm going to help you out. We are going to straighten it out. Don't worry about it."

I trusted him and got into his car. I felt this guy was really an angel, because if he hadn't pulled over, at the time of my prayer for clemency, I might have been attacked. He could have just passed by or I could have said, "No thanks, I'll just keep walking." But I believed that God forgave me, so thankfully, we both made the right divinely inspired decisions.

The man took me to his friend's house. This was the home of a medical doctor and the house was enormous. The property included a well-furnished guesthouse. My new friend, whom I believe was sent by God, left me in the guesthouse saying, "Chill here. In the morning we will send for a cab to take you into town, get your money, and then get you to the airport."

The owners of the house fed me and treated me like family. I offered them my last five dollars the next day when the taxi was arriving; but they refused. I was finally able to get enough money wired to me so I could buy a ticket home.

You can interpret this story however you want. I had made an agreement with God about not eating meat, but I ate it anyway, because I had felt hunger. I believe that God sent me on this side mission, because I broke my promise with Him. (If you are not a vegetarian and you haven't made that promise, it's a different thing.) I truly believe that eating animals is wrong and that my experience was a punishment or a test from God. He wanted me to get off the plane, walk that "highway of fear," and plead for His mercy – and then He sent it!

"It is better to leave everyone to his own way of thinking than begin an argument."
St. Thomas a Kempis

A Saving Arm

Chris Colvin

One summer day in downtown Cincinnati, a coworker and I were exiting the office together, busily chatting about our workday. We were on our routine path to the parking garage, approaching a crosswalk on 4th Street. We began to step off the curb, still chatting, naturally assuming that the other was paying attention.

Suddenly, out of nowhere, a strong and intentional female arm, reached in front of us and stopped us from stepping out into the street. Just then, a car sped by at a very high speed which would have, no doubt, seriously hurt, or possibly killed us.

We were both in a state of shock and so thankful for the Good Samaritan who had just saved our lives. We turned around to thank this stranger, but she was gone. She was nowhere in sight. I truly believe it was my Guardian Angel, as no mere human could have appeared and disappeared so quickly.

My friend and I continued our trek to the parking lot, rattled and astonished, and so thankful to be alive!

PART III

Touched by Heaven

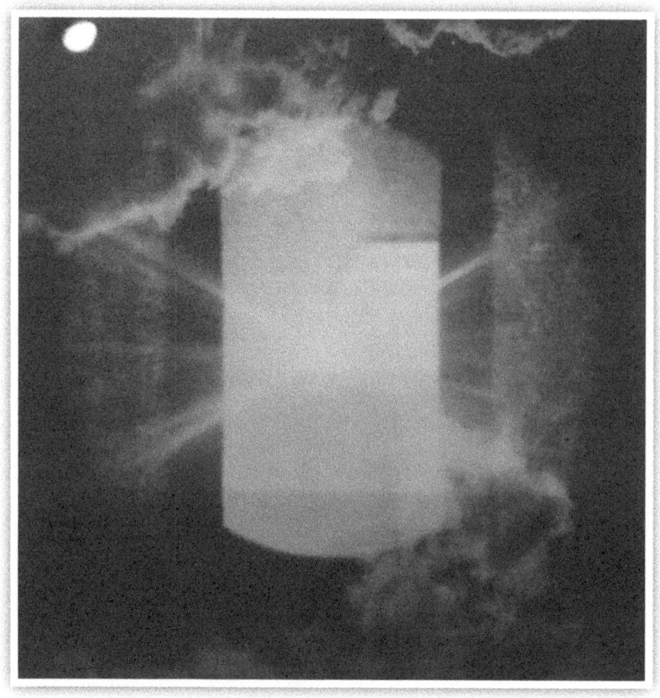

"Let them thank the Lord for such kindness, such wondrous deeds for mere mortals…" Psalm 107:15

"For we walk by faith, not by sight." 2 Corinthians 5:7

CHAPTER 8

Overcoming Loss, Adversity, and Satan's Attacks

"Let nothing disturb thee; Let nothing dismay thee. All things pass. God never changes. Patience attains all that it strives for. They who have God find they lack nothing. God alone suffices."
St. Theresa of Avila

"Finally, draw your strength from the Lord and from his mighty power. Put on the armor of God so that you may be able to stand firm against the tactics of the devil."
Ephesians 6:10-11

Beauty For Ashes

Alicia Brocker

October 13, 2016 was a cold day. It was the first day of autumn when it was cold enough to make a cozy fire in our wood-burning fireplace. My husband had the fire wood already piled up, and we had texted each other earlier that day, "Fire tonight!"

We were so excited to come home from work and warm up by it. It is one of my husband's favorite things to do.

Our home was already decorated top to bottom for Halloween. I couldn't wait to get off work, come home, and walk into the waft of pumpkin spice candles burning next to that warm, cozy fire.

Well.... we got our "fire" that night; just not the cozy one we had anticipated.

I was busy at work in the salon with a new client. The receptionist rushed into the shampoo room, where I was rinsing out color from my client's hair. "I'm so sorry to interrupt," she said apologetically, "It's your husband on the phone. He says it's an emergency."

My stomach sank. That nauseous feeling set in. He would never call the front desk unless it was a serious matter. I reached out for the phone. "What's wrong?" I said anxiously. He told me that our house was on fire and that the fire department was already on the way.

I was speechless; I didn't know what I'd be going home to! I apologized to my new client, "I'm so sorry, but I guess my house is on fire!" "Oh my gosh," she responded. "Don't worry about me! Go! Go!" I quickly gathered up my things and headed for home... or for what was left of it.

We had bought our home as a fixer-upper in April of 2015. It was a 1933 gem! It had loads of character, but it just needed some love. And that's what I did. I poured my heart into that home; decorating it and turning it into the cozy cottage I had first envisioned when we bought it. There were little projects still in the works, but we were nearly there. It was almost done...until that night.

During my frantic drive home, all I could think was, "Why, God? I worked so hard! Why would you take my home away from me?" I sobbed uncontrollably. I drove to the bottom of the road to turn onto our street, but couldn't. The entire street was blocked off! I had to park my car about fifteen houses down from ours. Those fifteen houses felt like a mile as I ran toward my beloved house!

It was like something out of a movie. Three or four large fire trucks, and several police cars, with lights flashing, were parked in our street. Several strangers were assembled in my yard! I remember thinking, "Who are these people? Get off my property!"

I went straight for my family and threw my arms around them. "Thank God we're all okay! That's what really matters!" As I wept, firefighters were bringing items that were possibly salvageable, onto my lawn. "My Memory Room!" I shouted to the firemen, "Please, get everything out of my Memory Room!" I was referring to our office on the first floor. It contained all of our most cherished things; such as my father's flag from his funeral, book collections, photo albums and all other irreplaceable items that really matter. I begged God to enable the firefighters to recover our keepsakes!

My phone kept buzzing in my back pocket. I remember taking my phone out, and looking to see who was calling. It was my insurance agent. I remember him kindly assuring us, "It's gonna be okay. I don't want to toss a bunch of numbers at you right now. But we're gonna take care of you. Don't worry; I'm on my way!"

Our warmhearted insurance agent drove an hour out of his way that night just to get to our home. He continued to assure us that we would be okay. He was wonderful, and we remain friends to this day.

Finally, the firefighters told us it was safe to walk back into our home. We'd been informed that the fire had started in my daughter's room on the second level. A spark from an electric outlet ignited her curtain, and that spark led to the raging fire. The fire grew and grew from there. Naturally, her room was the most damaged in the house.

I walked through the front door. Everything was black, dark, and wet. Pieces of the ceiling were falling as a result of the water that had been sprayed by the firefighters. I walked up the stairs and entered my daughter's room. It was like something out of a Halloween horror house. Black. Almost nothing was recognizable — all ashes. I saw shadows where she had carefully laid out her shoes the night before. I wept. My daughter had nothing left....or so I thought.

Our closest friends, our pastor, along with his wife, and the insurance agent all stood in a circle in what was left of our living room. My pastor led us in prayer as pieces of the ceiling continued to fall around us. I was all out of tears. A calmness came over me that was unexplainable. I heard the Holy Spirit repeat over and over in my head, "I will give you beauty for ashes. I will give you beauty for ashes."

Before they left that evening, I confided to the pastor's wife the message I had experienced from the Holy Spirit. I asked her, "Isn't there a scripture passage about beauty for ashes?" She confirmed, "There is! I'll send it to you!"

We slept in my mom's house that night, and in a hotel for the next ten days, until temporary living arrangements could be made. I laid my head down that first night on an air mattress next to my daughter, and couldn't stop thinking about what I had heard in my head: "Beauty for ashes." I just had to find that scripture passage! I got out my phone, and a quick Google search led me straight to it:

"...to bestow on them a crown of beauty instead of ashes, the oil of joy instead of mourning, and a garment of praise instead of a spirit of despair".
Isaiah 61:3 BSB

Peace came over me and I fell fast asleep.

My daughter had just turned twelve the week before the fire. The balloons from her birthday party, that had been in her room at the time of the fire, were no more. Now, she had nothing but the clothes on her back.

The "mom" in me went into survival mode. I went straight to a clothing store and tearfully, I told the sales staff, "I need help. I can't think. I just need a whole new wardrobe for my little girl." I explained what had happened and gave them her sizes. They went straight to work picking out the most beautiful clothes for my daughter.

Many people in our community donated clothes and accessories: purses, nail polish, and things every twelve-year-old girl would like to have. Word continued to spread quickly, and before we knew it, local boutiques had donated clothes as well. It was "Christmas in October" for my daughter. What a blessing! The generous outpouring was a humbling experience for my husband and me; being on the receiving end of donations was new to us. Our hearts were filled with gratitude to everyone who helped us in our time of need. God was certainly at work!

Over the next couple of days, we had to visit the ruins of our home, and try our best to take inventory of what belongings we had lost in the fire. This was especially difficult in my daughter's room where nothing was remotely recognizable. I had to stand in her room and think, at each location, what had been there. As I was looking through the ashes, I saw something that caught my eye. Something orange! Orange? In all this ashen blackness? I dusted it off and picked it up. It was her Bible!

Firefighters said the temperature in our house had reached over 1,500 degrees Fahrenheit. Her bed had melted down to the springs. And yet, out of the ashes, undamaged, I found her small Bible with pages as thin as tissue paper. Each page was totally intact. It was truly a miracle. I had indeed found BEAUTY IN THE MIDST OF ASHES!

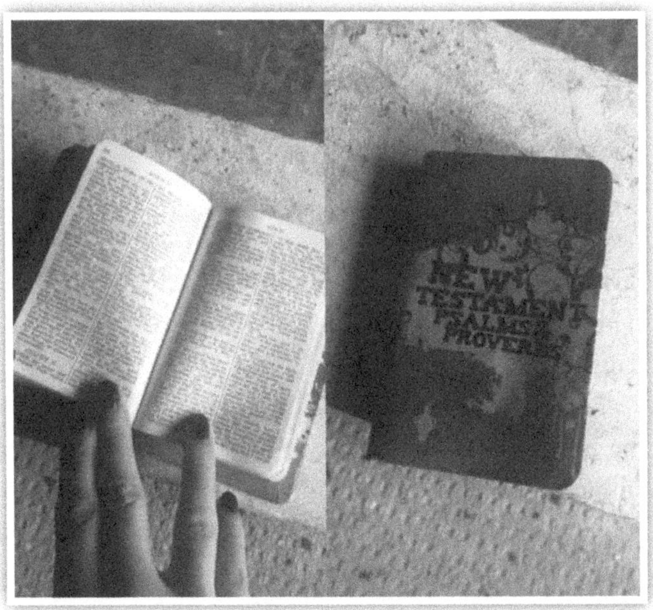

That was the first of many miracles for us. All of my most cherished objects in my "Memory Room" somehow stayed the driest and untouched by smoke. The restoration company was able to clean our treasures back to their original condition. Everything precious to me - all those things that "really mattered" had been salvaged!

I could see the light at the end of the tunnel; I would be coming home to a fully restored home. Since I love decorating, I enjoyed choosing new lighting, paint colors, floors, cabinets etc. After nine months to the day, on my father's birthday, our home was re-born, and I was finally ready to walk through the front door.

Beauty had indeed been resurrected from the ashes! Praise the Lord!

"Consider it all joy, my brothers, when you encounter various trials, for you know the testing of your faith produces perseverance." James 1:2-3

"A diamond is merely a lump of coal that did well under pressure."
Unknown

Everything is Possible

Char

My husband, Tom, died of colon cancer at the age of thirty-nine, in 1986. He left me with two precious children, Jamie and Michael; ages four and six.

While I was sitting in church for Tom's funeral Mass, with my two young children on either side of me, I saw Tom being lifted up to heaven between two angels. He was magnificent in glory, arms reaching up to heaven with a smile on his face that I will never forget. I knew, in that moment, that everything would be OK. My Tom was in the arms of God, and our life on earth would go on.

"In all circumstances give thanks, for this is the
will of God for you in Christ Jesus."
1 Thessalonians 5:18

We had owned a cleaning business at the time of his death. We had fifteen accounts, two employees, and were just starting to make money. By the grace of God, I was able to sell the business and stay home to raise my children. It was one of the greatest gifts God gave to me.

I dedicated my life to raising my daughter and son and helping them to become good Christians. We went every Tuesday evening, for two years, to a support group for grieving children. I believe this helped us quite a bit. It wasn't easy losing Tom, but with the help of God, prayer, my faith, family and friends, we made it through.

My children were six and eight when I prayed to God, and to Tom, and told them that I was ready to begin dating. My first date was with a man named Chris, and I never dated anyone else. We married five years after we began dating, and he was a wonderful father to my children. Chris died in 2017, at the age of seventy-one. We had been married for twenty-four years.

God was so good to let me have two incredible men in my life. We don't know the reasons why things happen, but we must accept them and know that God has a plan for all of us.

"For God did not give us a Spirit of cowardice but
rather of power and love and self-control."
2 Timothy 1:7

Our God is a good God, and I thank Him, every day, for the gifts He has bestowed upon me. I thank Him for my faith, and for knowing everything is possible for one who believes.

"I can do all things through God who strengthens me."
Philippians 4:13 NKJ

Two Miracles

Anonymous

I was diagnosed with breast cancer in 1991, and treated with radiation daily for six weeks and chemotherapy for six months. I was blessed with many wonderful friends to help with my children during the treatments. God was, and still is, so good to me!

Then in 2005, my mother passed away, and I did not take care of myself. I began eating junk food from the stress, and I continued eating this way for a few years. I did not exercise either and many bad habits were formed during those anxious years.

In 2009 I went to an oncologist to see about a hematoma that had developed on my breast after a minor car wreck and a fall. I got a mammogram and then a biopsy that determined I had a "slow growing cancer" in my right breast. So, I had developed breast cancer again, but not the same kind nor the same breast. My doctor also was concerned about a lump in the sentinel lymph node close to my underarm.

I was beating myself up about not taking care of my health. "I should have done this.... I should not have done that." I had these guilty thoughts on my mind day and night.

After finding out that I had cancer for a second time, we were at the funeral of a friend of mine who had just died of cancer. I was thinking, "How can I tell my friends that I have cancer when we are just now burying a friend who died of cancer?" I took my dilemma to a priest who suggested that I tell my friends, so that they could pray for me.

I had an appointment with my oncologist to talk over the next steps. I think he saw my depression and was trying to make me feel better by telling me, "This cancer is just something that older women get." He left the room, and the nurse came in to schedule appointments. Then, within two minutes, the doctor came back and sat down right in front of me and said, "I just want you to know that there is nothing you did to cause this and nothing you could have done to prevent this." Wow!

At that point I heard Jesus telling me, "I gave it to you. It's a gift!" I was finally able to breathe again.

Then came the operation to take all of the cancer out. After taking out the lump in my breast, the surgeon removed the sentinel lymph node close to my underarm. That lump was much bigger in size than they thought it would be. When they dissected the lump from my breast, they found that it was a slow growing cancer. But now, they couldn't understand how this sentinel lymph node was so big. It was bigger than the growth from my breast!

They looked at the lump from my breast more closely, dissecting it deeper, and found a fast-growing cancer covered by a slow growing cancer. The slow growing cancer protected me from the more serious cancer which could have taken over my whole body. The cancer had begun spreading into the lymph nodes, so they took out nineteen of them to make sure they got them all.

After all the operations, and chemo treatments, the surgeon told me I was cancer free!!!

Our daughter was in college in Austria for a semester at that same time. While there, she traveled around Europe on the weekends. The same day the surgeon told me I was cancer free, our daughter called me from Lourdes, France to tell me that she had just come out of the baths. She said that she had gone into the baths praying for me to be free of cancer! I told her about the news from the surgeon that I had received earlier that day.

I had received a miracle from our Lady of Lourdes, and I hadn't even been there!

"No trial has come to you but what is human. God is faithful and will not let you be tried beyond your strength; but with the trial He will also provide a way out, so that you may be able to bear it." 1 Corinthians 10:13

Satan Attacks and God Restores

Sue P.

My story begins at the end of July 2021, when my husband and I had contracted a severe case of COVID. By Thursday, August 5th we were both deathly sick, so my daughter called an ambulance that took us to the nearest hospital. I was given fluids, but they did nothing for my husband. They would not admit us, and told us we needed to find our own ride home, since we had come in the ambulance.

Thankfully we knew someone with a nice truck. He gave us a ride home in the back of his vehicle, since we didn't want to come in contact with him or his wife and possibly get them sick.

On Saturday, August 7th, the home health nurse came to assess our progress. She suggested I take my husband back to the hospital because his oxygen level was low. I drove him there that night. The next day I visited him and he seemed to be managing OK. On Monday, I arrived to visit him and the doctor said, "I'm sorry!" I asked her why she was apologizing. She said, "I'm sorry, your husband isn't going to make it!" I cried and ran out of the hospital.

That day, August 9th, was my husband's sixty-third birthday. I called him after I got home so my daughter and I could sing to him, wishing him a happy birthday. We were preparing to go visit him when he called us back a few minutes later, sobbing, saying the medical team was going to put him on the ventilator! I got the nurse on the phone, begging her to wait until I could get there to see him. She declined my appeal because they deemed it was an emergency. My husband's desperate phone call was the last time I talked to him. He died two days later.

My world was shattered! I was still sick and had major brain fog from COVID. I couldn't comprehend what had just happened! Everything from then on was a blur. Thankfully, my daughter and her family were able to stay with me for a while, to help take care of me and all of the funeral arrangements.

I began taking care of all the bills and changing everything over into my name. Let me tell you, that was a job! It took me two weeks just to get financial and legal matters put into place.

Shortly thereafter, I decided to put my house up for sale and move to North Carolina, where my daughter lived. In the meantime, I had to get my house in Arkansas ready to sell. I quit my job because I was still so sick and grieving. I couldn't imagine ever feeling capable of working again.

Then, everything that could go wrong did go wrong! I knew it was Satan trying to attack me and discourage me. I resolved to cling to Jesus all the more!

Here is where God showed Himself to me in a powerful way!

"In my distress I called out: LORD! I cried unto my God. From His temple He heard my voice; my cry to Him reached His ears." Psalm 18:7

It was time to begin packing, selling things, and working on my house before putting it up for sale. It seemed as though Satan was really trying to overwhelm me, because everything started breaking — and I mean everything!

One day my friend offered to cut my grass, but the riding lawn mower wouldn't work. When my neighbor came by, I asked him if he knew anything about those mowers. He said, "Let me look." He jumped on it and put it in full gear. It turned around quickly and crashed into my pull-behind metal wagon, ruining it. Then it turned the other way, and wrecked into my fence, and almost demolished it!

Later that day I went out to try the mower again, prayed...and it worked perfectly! I thanked God and praised Him for His loving kindness to me and His all-encompassing care for me.

A few days after the lawnmower disaster, I got on my tractor but the blade wouldn't turn. I was almost in tears, thinking, "Oh, no! How am I going to fix it?" I asked another neighbor to come and take a look at the problem. He said there was a pin missing off the shaft that turns the blades. He offered to pick one up for me and put it in place at no charge! I was ecstatic! Another answered prayer!

Not long after that, a friend borrowed my tractor to move some logs. While using it, he accidently cut the back two tires, dropped the front bucket, which hit the gate on my fence, and broke the fence post in two. I was convinced that all these mishaps were more harassments from Satan!

Wait. There's more!

My mailbox post was rotten at the bottom and about to fall over. My greenhouse door rotted and fell off, and my garage door opener wouldn't work.

Another project I had to tackle was using the blower to clean all the leaves away from my house. I filled it with gas and tried to start it but it locked up. I called my neighbor, who inspected it and said that it required mixed fuel. I had just ruined my eight-hundred-dollar blower! I nearly cried again, but then I thought, "Satan, get behind me. You will not win even if you take everything from me. I will still praise my Heavenly Father!"

"Then Job began to tear his cloak and cut off his hair. He cast himself prostrate upon the ground and said, 'Naked I came forth from my mother's womb, and naked shall I go back again. The Lord gave and the Lord has taken away; blessed be the name of the Lord!'" Job 1:20-22

I decided to fix my mailbox, front door and greenhouse door. A friend who lived nearly two hours away came to help. He bought and installed a new front door. We took the old front door and put it on the greenhouse. Then we fixed the mailbox post. Again, God came through and blessed me beyond all measure!

By this time, I was thanking God for providing for all my needs! He was showing me that He would continue to be my caregiver in my husband's absence! I started thinking of all the ways He had blessed and taken care of me since my husband had died and I began writing down all my blessings!

I looked in the Bible for every reference of "widow" mentioned therein. God promised to take care of the stranger, the fatherless and the widows! I was experiencing just that! Oh, if only we could recognize His goodness to us in the bad times as well as the good, and thank Him!

Once, again, my trials didn't stop.

There was a shampoo caddy in my bathroom shower which had poked a hole in the ceiling. I called a church member who was a construction worker, to ask him how much he would charge to fix it. He wouldn't quote a price on the phone, but did say he would come and work on it. He also fixed my garage door during the same visit. When he was finished, he charged me more than I had expected. I was actually shocked, but I graciously paid it. He asked me if I needed anything else done, and I said "No, thank you." I told him that I have friends who will come help me. I guess my response made him feel guilty, so he gave me $100 back. I told him "No, I hired you to do the job, and if that is what you charge, that is what I'll pay!" He insisted that I take the money, so I finally agreed!

A few days later, when I was cleaning out my closet, I noticed the ceiling had a two-foot crack all along the beam where the man had walked in my attic to repair the bathroom ceiling. I noticed another long crack in my living room. I called him and he told me how to fix it. I did my best and hoped it was good enough to sell the house. I was seeing how God was looking out for me!

"I praise the justice of the Lord; I celebrate the name of the Lord Most high." Psalms 7:18

After getting everything fixed on my property, I was ready to put my house up for sale. I prayed, asking God to take care of selling my house, if it was His will for me to move back with my family in North Carolina.

God connected me with two couples after church, who had been looking for property. I asked them what they were looking for, and they said, "Just land." So, I didn't mention I was selling my house to them at that time. The next week, when I saw them at church again, I asked them if they had found the land they had been seeking. They said they hadn't. This time I asked if they were interested in land with a house on it. They said, "Yes." That very morning, they came to look at my property. Two days later, they called me to report that they wished to purchase my house!

"...Blessed is your glorious name, and exalted above all blessing and praise." Nehemiah 9:5

I had never sold a house without a realtor, but God guided me through the whole process. I was even able to make a little more profit than I had originally anticipated. The new owners allowed me to live there until I was ready to move. They didn't even charge me rent! All I needed to do was pay for the electric, water, utilities, and garbage removal. I was able to stay there until I was ready to move to North Carolina to live with my daughter and her family. This was another amazing blessing!

God has watched over me through all my trials and He turned each trial into a blessing! I learned more about His love, and came closer to God through my losses! I serve such a wonderful and loving Heavenly Father! I cannot thank and praise Him enough!

"The Lord is my strength and my shield, in whom my heart trusted and found help. So, my heart rejoices; with my song I praise my God." Psalm 28:7

"Don't You Trust Me?"

Peggy B.

"I beg of Thee, Lord, to enlighten my understanding." Pope *Clement XI*

In September 2017, my friends and I were on our way to Medjugorje[11] to join Immaculee Ilibagiza on a pilgrimage. How excited we were! On the afternoon of the first day, September 8th, we decided to climb up Apparition Hill[2]. The way was steep and rocky beyond belief. My friend, Claire, noticed that I was struggling and said that I could go back down and wait until another day. I wavered but a quiet voice came to me and said, "Peggy, don't you trust me?" so I continued to climb.

There was a gentleman from Germany in the group ahead of us, and noticing my difficulty, handed me his cane to get over the steep rocks. When I offered to return it to him later, he told me to keep it.

We made our way up to the top by the statue of Our Blessed Mother. Each pilgrim found a perch on a rock and a private space to sit and pray. I was grateful for the gift of the cane while maneuvering over the rocks.

As we were getting ready to descend, someone directed us to a different path, saying it was an easier way down. Part of the way down the hill, a priest came over to bless my friends, who were a few feet away from me, and I was thinking "Darn, I didn't get blessed." Shortly after that, I watched my friends navigate the wet stones, fearing that they might slip and fall. Suddenly, I came upon a jagged rock and was concentrating on my next step.

Well, I don't remember that step, because in an instant I was lying on my back amid the rocks, and my left leg had a huge gash that was quickly swelling to the size of a golf ball. I also could not move because of the intense pain in my back.

Suddenly my friends, four strong men (who spoke only Polish), a Polish nurse (who did speak English) all surrounded me. The nurse gave me some water to drink and spoke to the men in Polish, instructing them how to handle me without causing more harm.

Within minutes I was picked up by two of the guys and carried down the rocky hill. Where else, but in Medjugorje, would you find a café at the bottom of a rocky path? The men carefully eased me into a chair as my friend went to hail a taxi. When the taxi arrived, the men picked me up, chair and all, and carried me through the crowds of people to the street.

I've never experienced the parting of the Red Sea, but let me tell you, the people who were on the walkway took one look at my bulging leg and stepped aside to make a clear path for the helpful men.

My friends cared for me, and the Aid Station did what they could for my leg. At the hotel, my friend, Sheila, stayed with me and prayed rosary after rosary with me while I rested in bed. Immaculee brought a beautiful crucifix for me to embrace while enduring the intense back pain.

Claire brought food to me and helped me dress. I got through the week with God's grace and the help of my angel companions, Claire, Sheila, Alice, Valentine, and Immaculee.

Eight days later, at home, I learned that I had suffered a T-12 compression fracture of my spine.

But the story doesn't end there. Do you remember the voice that said, "Peggy, don't you trust me?" Three months later, two weeks before Christmas, I was diagnosed with a very rare form of breast cancer. I was told to enjoy the holidays and deal with it in the new year.

After biopsies and a surgery to remove the tumor, a second surgery was required to clean up the edges and test the lymph nodes. As I was being prepped for this second surgery, an anesthesiologist entered my room and introduced himself as Thomas. He had an engaging smile and an accent which roused my curiosity. So, I asked him, "In which country were you born?" He immediately replied with a smile, "Rwanda." Little bells were going off in my head and I stated that I have a friend from Rwanda. Thomas asked me her name. I said "Immaculee Ilibagiza." Thomas broke into a bigger smile and said, "I know her too. We went to school together."

Then a voice said softly to me, "Do you trust me now, Peggy?" I answered, "Yes, Lord, you know that I do."

I went into surgery at peace, knowing that the Lord was directing all the caring hands around me. God is good all the time.

"Therefore, I ask in the abundance of Thy great
generosity that Thou may heal my sickness."
St. Thomas Aquinas

"But when he saw how strong the wind was, he became frightened, and beginning to sink, he cried out, 'Lord, save me.'" Matthew 14:30

God Connects the Dots

Paula S.

I am a cradle Catholic. I attended Catholic schools for twelve years. In elementary school I was very shy, but as I entered high school, I became sassy, selfish, and promiscuous. I should have been following in Jesus' footsteps, but I was a misguided, rebellious teenager who wanted to please myself and the boyfriends that crossed my path during this season of sinning.

"We know that the law is spiritual; but I am
carnal, sold into slavery of sin."
Romans 7:14

When I graduated from high school, I entered college to obtain my Associate's Degree in Fashion Merchandising. After achieving that degree, I started working in the retail business full time. Life was going pretty smoothly, but my sinful ways had never departed from me, and my social life was my main focus.

When I met Philip, the man who became my first husband, I thought my life was even better. He was also a cradle Catholic and we had so much in common. We were close in age, and our parents approved of our relationship. We were going to church together as a couple and he seemed to be my soul mate. We had a year-long engagement, with plans for a dream wedding in June 2000.

In March 2000, my sweet mother passed away from a pulmonary embolism at the age of fifty-seven. Life abruptly stopped for me. I didn't know how I was going to continue on without my mom. I wasn't even sure if I wanted to have our marriage ceremony in June. My father reminded me that everything was already paid for, and that my mother would want me to get married as we had planned.

At this point in my life, I didn't have a personal relationship with God. I had been stumbling around in life not caring what His plan was for me. I decided to take Dad's advice and followed through with the wedding. I was very concerned for my dad's welfare. He had not lived alone for over thirty-three years.

As my marriage progressed, I battled depression due to my mother's passing and guilt for leaving my father. My new husband was not very supportive of my mental health issues. He told me, "You need to get over it and move on."

I sought help from my family doctor who prescribed medicine for my depression and anxiety. My father passed away in June of 2002 from congestive heart failure at the age of sixty-one. So, I entered the grieving process all over again. Did I turn to God? No, I didn't!

In August of 2002, we became pregnant with our first child. My pregnancy was extremely difficult and I was in and out of the hospital with chronic morning sickness and dehydration. I really thought God was angry with me and that He was paying me back for living my life the way I had been living it.

"For I know well the plans I have in mind for you, says the Lord, plans for your welfare, not for your woe; plans to give you a future full of hope." Jeremiah 29:11

In May of 2003, Philip and I welcomed our daughter, Mallory, and my dream had come true! What a glorious day that was for me. Motherhood agreed with me, but unfortunately, marriage did not. Philip served me with divorce papers in June, 2005.

As a single mother, I should have turned to God, but once again, I didn't. Instead, I turned to dating. I met Michael, and it was a turbulent, toxic relationship. For some reason, I thought he needed me and I was there to fix him. I was so broken and lost myself; how in the world could I fix someone else?

"Why do you notice the splinter in your brother's eye, but do not perceive the wooden beam in your own eye? How can you say to your brother, 'Let me remove that splinter from your eye,' while the wooden beam is in your eye." Matthew 7:3-5

This verse was a real eye opener for me. (Pardon the pun.)

In September 2007, Michael and I welcomed our daughter, Marlena, and once again I was happy. Unfortunately, Michael and I were not married, or even dating, at the time she was born.

Single motherhood had become the norm for me; I decided that I didn't need a man to take care of me and my daughters. God is the almighty provider, so I didn't date for two years. Who had time for dating with two small children and a full-time job?

My friend set me up with a male friend of hers, and we went on a couple of dates. I didn't realize he was a snake slithering into my life; preying upon an overworked single mother that he thought needed to be saved. When I discovered I was pregnant, he asked me to get an abortion. I was, and still am, pro-life, and that was never going to happen. Then I found out that he had a wife and seven children in another state!

I had the hardest decision to make for my daughters, my unborn baby, and me. I contacted Catholic Charities and went through the adoption process. God led me to two wonderful people who adopted my son.

I began to get to know God and His word. I have faithfully been reading and studying the Bible for the past eleven years, and now it is the guidebook for my life.

"Come to me, all you who labor and are burdened,
and I will give you rest." Matthew 11:28

"Will You Suffer for Me?"

Julie Fortner

Have you ever wondered if God is really talking to you or if it is something you are just imagining? Well, that happened to me in the summer of 2016. One beautiful summer morning I was sitting in Adoration[1], praying, when I heard a voice say to me, "Will you suffer for me?"

I turned around to see who said that, but no one was there. In fact, no one was anywhere near me, and I seemed to be the only one in the church at that time. I know I heard a soft, audible voice whisper, "Will you suffer for me?" It only happened once. I didn't answer the question, so I thought perhaps I had imagined the voice. I didn't share this experience with anyone at that time.

Later that year, my daughter was flying home and told me that she had an incredible experience on the plane. She had a vision of me in a loving embrace with Our Lady and my daughter had so much peace about her experience with the vision. It was then that I realized I hadn't imagined what I had heard that summer in the Adoration Chapel. The Lord had been asking me to suffer for Him. I didn't know when, why or how; I just knew something was going to happen. I still wasn't planning to tell anyone what was going through my mind.

On January 7, 2017, I began to get a tingling sensation in my feet and legs. I felt like they were falling asleep. As I moved around, the feeling wouldn't go away; instead, it was spreading higher up my body. My first thought was that I was experiencing shingles. I was aware that there was a shot I could have administered within the first twenty-four hours of the symptoms of shingles, and that would aid in healing the malady. I planned to wait until the next morning to see how I felt.

At 4:17 a.m., I woke up with the tingling sensation still there. It was too early to go to the doctor's office for the shingles shot, so I thought God must need me to pray for someone. So, that is what I did. Then I fell right back to sleep. I woke up again at 7:00 a.m. with my symptoms still present, so my husband and I decided to go to the hospital.

We arrived at 8:00 a.m. on Sunday morning, January 8, to an empty emergency room. The only other people present were finishing with their check-in and we were next. That never happens! It's usually an all-day process! We were subsequently checked in and escorted to an "emergency room suite" within twenty minutes. Not long after we were settled into the room, the doctors came in to see what was happening with me. They decided to start with an MRI on my spine.

Everything was happening so fast! By 10:30 a.m. we had the results. The radiologist had seen a mass on my spine, but they couldn't identify what it was. I had another scan of my brain, but luckily, that was clear. By now it was just past lunch, and a team of doctors were discussing my case. After doing some research they thought I had something called transverse myelitis. This condition is very rare.

Transverse Myelitis occurs when a virus attacks the spinal column. In my case, the virus ate away the myelin sheath around my spine between the T5 and T8 vertebrae, thus exposing all of my nerve endings from my ribs and below. Basically, the communication from my brain to my torso and legs was broken.

When we asked what we should expect from this diagnosis, their response was quite vague. They said I had a 33% chance of getting better, a 33% chance of staying the same and a 33% chance of getting worse and never being able to walk again. They also said that it could eventually go to my brain and kill me.

So really, they had no idea what was going to happen to me. They wanted to run some more tests, so they admitted me into the hospital for three days. They also gave me high doses of steroids to kill the virus and they warned me that I would have some bad side effects. However, I had no side effects at all!

It was at this point that I told my husband what had happened in Adoration six months earlier. Convinced that this was something God was asking me to do, I made a deal with God! I told Him that I would endure this suffering if no one could see my pain, and instead, all they would see was joy emanating from me.

We contacted one of our friends to tell them what was happening, and she proceeded to tell me that her son's father-in-law had passed away during the night. I asked her what time this had happened, and she said he had died at 4:17 a.m. in the morning. That was the exact time I had woken up and offered my sufferings for God's intentions! It was then that I knew I was on a mission for God.

While I was in the hospital for those three days, I was losing my ability to walk and stay balanced. Whenever I put my feet on the ground, it felt like I was walking barefoot on a bed of nails. My feet were in a lot of pain and always felt cold to me. During the middle of the night, I had a sensation that someone was massaging my feet. When I looked around, no one was in the room, but my feet were being rubbed. I said to myself, "If this is my Angel, please don't stop rubbing my feet." The sensation did not go away, and I fell peacefully back to sleep.

Many miraculous things happened during the next six months. I lost all my abilities to function from my ribs down. I was in a wheelchair from January 22, 2017 until March 1, 2017. I couldn't drive for three months. Yet, I managed to make it to daily Mass everyday as I had scheduled my therapy around Mass time. My friends and family drove me to therapy and then Mass. If they couldn't stay for Mass, then someone at church would take me home. I am a Eucharist Minister[7] and I continued, with the blessing of our priest, to distribute communion from my wheelchair and later with my cane, both at daily Mass and at Sunday Mass.

Whenever I would get shooting pains, I would stop what I was doing and say, "I have to pray now." The pains were my sign that God needed me to pray for someone at that very moment. I remember one specific time my husband and I were going for a walk and I got a tremendous sensation of pain throughout my body and I stopped and said, "We have to pray right now. I'm not sure why but something is wrong, and we just have to pray." I offered up my sufferings and we said a short prayer for the person God needed us to pray for. The pain subsided after our prayer. An hour and a half later we found out that at the very moment we were praying, a friend of mine lost her fifteen-year-old niece in a tragic accident.

Sometimes I would lay in bed at night with the pain so intense I couldn't sleep, so I would tell the Lord to give me the pain of those that couldn't handle it, because with His graces I could suffer for them. Eventually the pain would subside and I would sleep peacefully.

A friend of mine lost her husband during this six-month period. On the day she was going to see his body for the first time after his death, I spoke to her just before she left. I told her that I was going to Adoration and I would be praying for her. During the entire time in Adoration, I was sobbing uncontrollably as I was offering up my prayers for her. The sobbing stopped the minute I left the chapel. I asked her how her visit went. She said, "It was beautiful. I had so much peace."

My husband had just started a three-year Deacon Formation program in our diocese in the fall of 2016. During the semester I got sick, he was studying what it meant to have a deacon's heart and to serve. He later told me how much my illness and suffering formed him into the deacon he is today. He was working full-time at a major consumer goods company, and was planning to work there for another five years. However, he took a three-month leave of absence to care for me. It was during this absence that he experienced a changed heart.

My husband's job required him to outsource a lot of his business, but he did not want to outsource my care. He took me to therapy a couple of days each week and he helped me in the middle of the night when I had to go to the bathroom. He helped me in and out of the car when I was in my wheelchair. This is when my husband truly learned to serve.

He believes God used my illness to empty himself and give up his identity as an executive. He retired early, so he could focus full-time on ministry work as a deacon. He would probably still be working to this day if God hadn't intervened. Just think of how much worthwhile ministry work he would have missed!

People would often say to me, "You are so joyful!" This occurred most often when I was in the wheelchair. When I could walk again, and no longer needed the wheelchair, people would ask if I was cured, because they couldn't see my pain. God has a funny sense of humor! Be careful what you ask for! But be happy to serve Him, whatever His plan!

Six and a half years after I contracted transverse myelitis, I still have a slight chronic tingling on the bottom of my feet, which I choose to joyfully accept, as a reminder of God's infinite love for me; as I said, "YES," (finally) to his question "Will you suffer for me?"

"The God of all grace who called you to His eternal glory through Christ will Himself restore, confirm, strengthen, and establish you after you have suffered a little." 1 Peter 5:10

CHAPTER 9

The Power of Prayer

"So let us confidently approach the throne of grace to receive mercy and to find grace for timely help." Hebrews 4:16

"In the same way, the Spirit too comes to the aid of our weaknesses; for we do not know how to pray as we ought, but the Spirit itself intercedes with inexpressible groanings." Romans 8:26

"Maria Goretti, Pray for Me"

Claire Patterson

I was a very naive twenty-year-old young lady on vacation without my parents for the first time. I had traveled with four other young women to Paradise Island in the Bahamas. While relaxing by the hotel pool, reading my economics text, a very handsome young man sat in the chair next to me and introduced himself as "John." He said that he and his family lived on the island. I was flattered by his attention and enjoyed our conversation. When he asked if I wanted to take a boat ride around the island with him, I agreed to go.

John walked to the parking lot to get his car while I gathered my things. Regretfully, I didn't bother to tell my friends where I was going. He pulled up to the hotel entrance in a very nice red convertible. We drove to a local harbor where he was recognized by the gate attendant. After walking along the pier, John helped me into what seemed to be a small yacht. There was a lot of room on deck with steps leading to a floor below, where I assumed were the living quarters. I imagined that his family was very well to do.

When we motored out into the water, far away from any shore, he began to undress and expected me to do the same. When I explained that I was a virgin, and planned on staying that way, he became angry. John said that when I had agreed to a boat ride, I had also agreed to sex, just like every other girl he'd been with. This man was used to getting anything he wanted, and did not handle rejection well.

I told him that I had only agreed to a boat ride and nothing more, and demanded that he take me back to my hotel immediately. He refused. He threatened to rape or beat the living (insert cuss word) out of me. He said there was nothing I could do about it.

As I tried pulling up the anchor, he suddenly picked me up and threw me overboard. I was startled and afraid, but I was too far from land to swim anywhere safely. There was no other option than to climb up the ladder he had lowered for me.

At that point I began praying, with all my heart, to St. Maria Goretti[24] for her intervention. "Please pray for me, Maria. Help me to be as strong and as brave as you were. Ask God to help me now!"

Maria and God answered my prayer immediately. The man suddenly stopped threatening me, put his clothes back on, pulled up the anchor and headed back to my hotel.

As we were approaching the dock adjacent to where I was staying, John asked if he could take me to dinner that night. I was flabbergasted and didn't even respond to him.

I performed an Olympian long-jump from the deck of the boat to the pier before he even had a chance to secure it to the dock. I ran all the way back to the hotel and went straight to my room to take a shower.

I was too embarrassed by my foolishness and naiveté, that I never mentioned this episode to my traveling companions. I did share it with my Mom after arriving home, and a handful of people since.

I have never forgotten St. Maria Goretti's powerful and effective intervention and protection.

"Do not fear the king of Babylon, before whom you are now afraid; do not fear him, says the Lord, for I am with you to save you, to rescue you from his power."
Jeremiah 42:11

"If You are Real, Show Me!"

Mark Brockman

I am a jail ministry volunteer for Catholic Charities. I visit inmates once a month in Northern Kentucky and have participated in this mission for three and a half years. There has not been a time when I depart from visiting these folks, that I don't feel overcome with the presence of God and the Holy Spirit. These people, surprisingly, often have a good knowledge of the Bible along with a great passion for the welfare of their fellow inmates. It is a great blessing to speak about God and His wondrous works with them, God's children. The Holy Spirit truly is guiding me in this ministry.

A strong example of God's presence in the prison occurred recently during one of my visits. Normally we have a ratio of two volunteers meeting with three to ten inmates. This particular night we had three volunteers and one inmate. While walking to the gathering space to meet with this person, I was apprehensive due to the fact that there would be three of us, and only one inmate. I didn't want the prisoner to feel outnumbered by our group. After our introductions, however, this meeting quickly took a significant turn.

The inmate, within the first three minutes, relayed to us that he had recently come into this jail system and had spent the first four days in solitary confinement. He had dealt with voices in his head for many years, and shared with us that being in solitary confinement was the most difficult thing he had ever experienced.

By the fourth day of his confinement, he couldn't take it anymore and screamed out to God, "If You are real, show me!" It was only a few minutes before the door was opened by an officer to release him from his solitary cell.

As he relayed this story tears rolled down his face. I was tearing up myself, as were the other two volunteers. To say God was in our presence is an understatement! Needless to say, the rest of our visit was very special. The inmate also shared with us that his daughter, who is in a Catholic grade school, is making special bracelets to sell and raise money to help pay for her father's legal expenses. Wow!

What a wonderful evening we all shared in the manifest presence of God and the Holy Spirit! This touching experience will always stay with me. I am constantly thanking the good Lord for placing me in this ministry, and I pray that I can give as much as I receive from these special people.

"The Spirit of the Lord is upon me, because He has anointed me to proclaim good news to the poor. He has sent me to proclaim liberty to the captives and recovering of sight to the blind, to set at liberty those who are oppressed." Luke 4:18

A Close Call

Joe Gering

In 1968 I received my military draft number; 42. I delayed my entry into the service by going to college for a couple of years, but I gave up my deferment in 1971, so I was obligated to serve for two years with no guarantees.

The Army decided I was to be trained as a "Military Police Dog Handler". My original orders were to go to Vietnam. By all reports, a dog handler's life expectancy in Vietnam was not very long. Naturally, I was not happy about the situation. However, I had already surrendered my will to God the Father. I said that I would accept whatever came my way during my military service. I just asked Him to please guide me to do His will. Mom never stopped praying for my safety.

About a week before I was scheduled to ship out, my orders were changed, and I was sent to Korea. It was classified as a "hardship tour," but it was much safer than Vietnam would have been at that time.

During my years in the Army, I was involved in many life-saving and life-changing experiences. Through these tough times and trials, I learned that God is aware of and involved in everything I am confronted with every moment of every day. The Father always has a plan for each of us.

The Father, with Jesus, the Holy Spirit, Mary, the angels, and the saints is always with me to guide and help me through any difficulty. I know I must surrender to the Father's will, pray, and listen for His voice.

"God indeed is my savior; I am confident and unafraid. My strength and courage is the Lord, and He has been my savior." Isaiah 12:2

Prayer Works

Anonymous

In 1958, I was seven years old and living in Parma, Ohio. One day my mom was getting ready to go out with my dad to a party. As she was showering, she got a terrible headache. My dad contacted our doctor, who came over and prescribed medicine to reduce Mom's pain. The doctor came back every day for a week, then finally admitted her to the hospital for tests. She was diagnosed with a cerebral hemorrhage which would require a dangerous operation to reach the bleeding and stop it. The surgeon told us that Mom had only a fifty percent chance of surviving the operation.

Since I was the oldest boy in the family, my dad took me to the hospital with him. As we traveled back home, Dad told me that if Mom dies, all six of us kids would have to go to an orphanage, because he alone could not take care of us.

At that moment, I started to pray for Mom's survival.

The surgery was successful and Mom recovered. She cared for us for the next eight years; at which time she passed away suddenly from an aneurysm. Although there were seven of us kids at that time, four of us were teenagers. We were blessed to be old enough to care for one another and our three-year-old brother.

I thank God for answering my prayers and giving us time to grow up before my Mom passed away. God is good!

"And we have this confidence in Him, that if we ask anything according to His will, He hears us. And if we know that He hears us in whatever we ask, we know that what we have asked Him for is ours." 1 John 5:14-15

Relief from Depression

Joe Gering

Around 1986 I had three young children. My wife and I agreed that she should stay home with our kids, and I would work. Money was tight and always a concern.

One evening, on my way home from an appointment, I stopped at a store to pick up a few items. While I was in the checkout line, a stranger came up to me and said, "God just flashed me a message to give to you. You should not worry about money. I don't know anything else about your situation, but that is the message." I was startled and didn't know what to make of it. A minute or two later I looked for the man, but he was nowhere to be found.

Even after this message, I was still concerned about having enough money to cover the bills, but by the grace of God, we always seemed to have enough income to cover expenses after that incident.

"My God will fully supply whatever you need, in accord with his glorious riches in Christ Jesus."
Philippians 4:19

I didn't realize it at the time, but I had started to suffer from depression in the late 1990's. After I was diagnosed, I started taking medication and continued this therapy for about ten years. It was a rough period in my life, but God always seemed to send me special help when I needed it the most.

Fr. Joe, a priest I knew from my days in high school, was a special instrument of God. He was my spiritual director. Somehow, whenever I was really struggling, he would be sent to my town. He was a great source of hope for me.

Then I discovered Our Lady of the Holy Spirit Center[18] and joined Duke and Claire Patterson's rosary group. Praying together each week was a great source of peace for me. Quite often, upon my return home from the rosary group, I would find a message on my voice mail leading to a new business offer. This always happened when I really needed it.

Another lesson of how God was always there for me came around 2005. None of our regular prayer group was going to be able to make it for rosary at Our Lady of the Holy Spirit Center one particular evening. I planned to stay home, but something kept gnawing at me all afternoon to go. So, at the last minute, I walked out the door, even though I thought I would be the only one there. To my surprise, four other people, who only attended sporadically, also showed up. If I had not followed the Holy Spirit's silent nudge to go, the other four couldn't have gotten into our prayer room, as I was the only one who knew the keycode.

One evening during our rosary group, I asked Duke if he would take my rosaries to be blessed by Mary. Duke instructed me to put them by Mary's statue. After rosary, Duke said that Mary had been with us and she had blessed my rosaries in a way that he had never heard before; she sang the blessing! (At that time no one in our group knew that I was a singer.)

If I had ever doubted that Mary, and all of heaven, was there on a very personal level for each one of us, I never doubted it again.

"Have no anxiety at all, but in everything, by prayer and petition, with thanksgiving, make your requests known to God. Then the peace of God that surpasses all understanding will guard your hearts and minds in Jesus Christ." Philippians 4:6-7

Are Prayers of Petition Useless?

Anonymous

In the early 1970's, I took a theology class from a charismatic, extremely intelligent priest professor. He explained an intriguing theory that God created us with a free will which by its nature precluded God from interfering with the working of the natural world. The world and man functioned in an evolution toward God designed by God at creation. He taught that prayers of petitions did nothing other than serve as psychological crutches to bring comfort to the petitioner. He proposed that God was not going to interfere with the natural world by answering prayer requests; that would negate our free will. He believed that prayers of praise, gratitude and contrition were the only worthwhile prayers.

Because I had had lots of prayers of petition go unanswered, from my perception, Father's explanation rang true to me, and I fell for it. I quit asking God for favors. Prayers of praise, thanksgiving and contrition were my only prayers.

A few years later, married and with a twelve-month-old, I felt called to investigate fostering infants for the time between their release from the hospital until arriving at their loving, forever home. We were told that the time period we would have the infant was usually about two weeks. I figured we could help a number of infants until God would hopefully bless us with our second pregnancy.

Our first little guy stayed with us for almost <u>four</u> months! My brother's wedding was coming up. My husband and I were both in the wedding party. Out-of-town cousins, two young couples and one single girl, were coming to stay with us. They would sleep on the living room floor, a sofa, and bunk beds, which were in the infant's room. Additionally, my husband was completely redoing our kitchen. It was practically gutted with the stove smack in the middle of the room, and no microwave available.

Weeks before, we had told the Sister handling our case, about our need <u>not</u> to be fostering at the time of the wedding. She thought that was reasonable and doable. It was getting awfully close to the wedding, and the baby's father was going back on his decision to relinquish his son. I was beside myself worrying about handling it all: a colicky, high maintenance, little guy, a toddler, house guests without a working kitchen, and both my husband and I in the wedding party. How were we going to swing this? Although I hadn't prayed to God for a favor since college, in my state of anxiety I said to God one night, "Lord, we are trying to do your will caring for Your little son, but this is too much. Please get his case settled very soon."

The next morning, Sister tracked me down, as I sat in the dentist chair, to tell me to bring the baby in ASAP. The birthfather was cooperating, and the adoptive parents were coming in a matter of hours.

I was sad to say good-by to our little buster of a boy, but also relieved that we could handle the wedding now. I didn't think to thank God for making it happen. I only praised Him because it all worked out.

The first preemie we had was *very* tiny! She needed to eat every two hours around the clock. I had to wake her up for feedings even if she was sleeping soundly. One week after she had arrived, I found out I was pregnant. My morning sickness came soon thereafter, and was worse at night. It had been my idea to take in foster infants, because I felt I should be doing more. Our son was a very easy child to parent. Going from a full-time job in a large busy hospital to caring for one compliant little boy didn't seem to be enough. However, my husband's situation was completely opposite. Having my husband take the night feedings was not going to work. He left for work at 6:15 a.m. and returned about 5:30 p.m. Then he'd change out of his dress clothes and resume whatever repair/remodeling job he was currently working on. He always helped with the dishes and bedtimes, however.

The morning sickness made it miserable to sit in the rocker in the middle of the night, trying to feed a preemie who didn't want to eat. Tearfully, I said to the Lord, "Please God, help me here, You gotta do something!" Low and behold! Sister called the very next day. I was to bring the infant in that day, as Sister was placing that tiny little girl with her anxious new parents!

Now I was two for two. Twice I had asked God for help, and twice my request was answered immediately! Was this really "coincidence" as my college professor would have said, or was God actually intervening in my life to answer my prayers? I decided on the latter.

In late 1980, newly pregnant with #3, I committed to be on our diocese's first women's Christ Renews His Parish[4] Team. I said I would take any role *except* witness! Listening to the Holy Spirit was not something I did well. The whole team, though, ended up putting their hands on my shoulders and praying. They were certain that God wanted me to do the "God's Loving Care" witness, and that settled that.

As our formation progressed, so did my pregnancy. At the Renewal weekend I was eight months pregnant.

I was carrying a big baby, and he was positioned transverse; head on my left side, feet on the right. Because he was big at this late stage of pregnancy, the doctor said he was "wedged" so tightly that there was little chance the baby would change position. We had to take C-section classes because the doctor was so certain it would be a C-section. My team was always praying for the baby and me.

The retreat had begun and it was time for me to give my witness. Calmly, (only by God's answer to everyone's prayers) I spoke. I told the story of my theology professor's explanation as to why prayers of petition were only psychological crutches for us. He theorized that God does not intervene in our lives and interfere with the free will He'd given to us. He believed that God does not grant prayer requests. Then I witnessed to my dramatic change of thinking when both my requests pertaining to the foster infants were answered immediately. I told my audience that I now believe in the power of prayers of petition.

As soon as the witness was over, a woman came rushing up to me. I didn't know her, but I did recognize her from college. Through tears, she shared with me that after taking the same class with the same priest professor, she had accepted the belief in the futility of prayers of petition. My witness was the confirmation she needed to restore her faith that God does indeed intervene in our lives in answer to our prayers. She was overjoyed and so was I!

I went back to the chair at my table. I felt what I figured was my stomach doing flip flops from the extremely emotional event I had just experienced. It was lunch time, and as we all stood up, I felt a strange sensation in my abdomen, but didn't think anything of it. I was excited, pregnant and hungry, after all. My friend, who sat next to me said I looked thinner to her. At that moment, my husband walked in to serve our lunch. He saw me and excitedly said the baby must have moved, because my abdomen was shaped completely different. I felt my abdomen with my hands, and sure enough the baby had moved to a more beneficial position! My baby started turning just as I had finished my witness, and my team all thanked God!

Two days later my doctor was quite surprised to see the baby's head down, and soon our baby was born with no complications. Praise God!

"It *(Love) bears all things, believes all things,*
hopes all things, endures all things."
1 Corinthians 13:7

A Broken Arm

Mary Anne Gronotte

I was a little four-year-old girl in 1951, when our family went to the Drive-In for a movie night. There was a playground in front of the screen for all the kids to enjoy before the movie started.

I was on the big slide. I probably shouldn't have been on it, but my big brother was there to keep me safe. I must have caught my arm on the bars before sliding down, because the next morning my arm really hurt a lot. I didn't want to tell my mom because she had other little kids to take care of and she was always busy.

I had a statue of the Virgin Mary on top of my chest-of-drawers, and sometimes we would put peony flowers in a vase there in the summer. I remembered that they always smelled so good.

So, I knelt down in front of my statue and prayed out loud to Mary, "Please help my arm feel better. It really hurts bad." Just as I was praying, my mother walked by my bedroom door and overheard my prayer. Mother Mary had arranged this for me.

Mom took me to the doctor's office and had my arm x-rayed. I did have a broken arm! Our Blessed Mother did make it feel better! She had answered my prayer.

St. Therese and the Roses

Anonymous

My story starts several years ago, when I developed a friendship with St. Therese of Lisieux.[27] I have always had a devotion to many saints over the years, but I was fascinated with Therese. I love the "little way" she lived her life. Her vocation was love. She spent her twenty-four short years of life isolated, nine years of which were behind the walls of the Carmelite Convent, and yet she became a Doctor of the Catholic Church[6].

Pope St. Pius X called her, "the greatest saint of modern times." Therese's autobiography, The Story of a Soul, has allowed the world to understand the holiness of this saint. She is continuously true to her promise: "I will send down a shower of roses from the heavens. I will spend my heaven doing good on earth."

My wife and I know a family who has a daughter with cystic fibrosis. To ensure her privacy, I will refer to this person as "Lily." Lily is a young teenager with a beautiful smile and a beautiful spirit. She did not let her illness affect her life. Her story touched my heart.

We are so helpless in these situations, and all we can do is pray. I decided to call on my friend, St. Therese. I challenged my special saint to heal Lily, if it was our Lord's will. I promised that I would daily pray to Therese and asked for complete healing for Lily.

Venerable Bishop Fulton Sheen says, "If you are going to ask for a miracle, you might as well ask for a big one."

I prayed three prayers to St. Therese daily: the "Novena Rose Prayer," the "Miraculous Invocation to St Therese," and a "Novena to Therese." These prayers for Lily greatly increased my love and devotion to St. Therese. I was faithful to these prayers for a couple of years.

Lily continued her journey in life with no complaints; just living her life to the fullest. Her life expectancy was twenty-five to thirty years. I can't imagine being given that kind of prognosis at that age, but she persevered.

This story takes a different twist here. A few years ago, I was going to daily Mass. There was a lady who always sat in the pew behind me. She wore a veil and I could tell she was very devout. For the longest time, I never met her.

I had also started another prayer to St. Therese at that time. During this set of prayers, I said the "Glory Be to the Father" prayer twenty-four times in honor of the twenty-four years that St. Therese lived. After each "Glory Be," I prayed, "St. Therese of the Child Jesus, pray for us."

As I started this new set of prayers, I asked for a sign from Therese that she was hearing my prayers. I said, "You send roses to so many people; send one to me." Since I am a man, I thought my chance of getting a rose from someone would be slim. I mean, who sends a rose to a man?

On the fourth day of this twenty-four-day novena, I went to 10:00 a.m. Mass as usual. The lady who sat in the pew behind me was there as usual. As Mass was concluding, I received a tap on my shoulder. The lady in the pew behind me gave me an envelope. I asked her, "What is it?" She just said, "It's for you." I said, "Thanks," and went to the back of the church. My curiosity got the better of me and I opened the envelope. There was a card with forty dollars in it. The lady was still in her pew praying. I went back to her and introduced myself and thanked her for the money. I asked her, "Why are you giving me money?" She said, "I just want to do something nice for you. You can do whatever you want with it." She said she enjoyed seeing me at daily Mass every day. We talked for a while and then I left.

As I got home from Mass, I sat down to say my daily prayers. I started my twenty-four-day novena to Therese. Halfway through my prayer, I realized that I had not even read the card that the lady had given me. I picked it up and started reading and looking at it. My jaw dropped. Do you remember that I had asked Therese for a rose as a sign that she had heard my prayer?

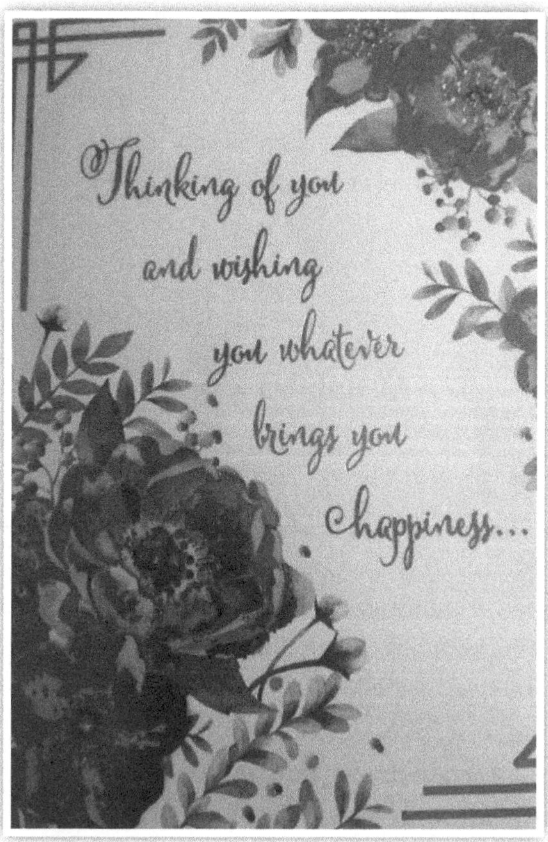

The card had THIRTEEN roses on it! I sat there in amazement that Therese had given me this sign. Coincidence or St. Therese? I choose Therese. I knew then that St. Therese had heard my prayer and she was taking care of Lily on our Lord's terms.

In conclusion: What are the odds that I would ask for a rose from Therese as a sign that she is hearing my prayers? And what are the odds that a lady in church, whom I had never met, would give me a card with thirteen roses on it? Therese and God work in amazing ways!

I spoke with Lily's mother earlier this year. She said they have made medical advances with cystic fibrosis. Lily's lifespan has now been increased to forty-five to fifty years. Thanks to Therese and to Our Lord for hearing my prayers!

"May the God of hope fill you with all joy and peace in believing, so that you may abound in hope by the power of the Holy Spirit." Romans 15:13

A Whale of a Prayer

Anne Rose

Have you ever prayed for a whale to roll over? I have—on a whale watch off the shores of Cape Cod.

There were no guarantees on this "Jonahesque" voyage that we would even come near a whale in all that ocean. Yet, as we approached the open sea, my heart leapt just thinking about the possibilities. "Look for the spouting mist, or birds hovering about looking for fish, or look for the luminescence of the whale's undersides," we were told.

Relentlessly, the steel-hulled vessel plowed the deep sea, leaving miles of white foam in its wake. But no sightings—just waves glistening in the blinding sun. Until a distant geyser appeared. And then, a long black form slipped above the waves. This sighting of a minke whale stirred me to the point that, like Peter at the Transfiguration, I felt compelled to say something! "God, let these whales give you glory. And let me see it." Somehow, I knew I would.

But seeing was not that easy, since two hundred and twenty passengers were packed into this boat like tuna after a good haul. And now minke, finback and humpback whales were all appearing out of the blue. I had to get a better look. So, squeezing through the huddled mass of amateur photographers, I made my way onto the pulpit of the boat to catch a glimpse of two humpbacks' enormous ruffled-edged tail fins waving as they dove.

After I had seen enough to satisfy my curiosity, I stepped down to allow others to get a better look. Almost immediately, the tour guide excitedly announced that the humpbacks had resurfaced, demonstrating breaching and fin slapping behavior off the starboard side. (No good deed goes unpunished.) Suddenly, due to the stampede of passengers, the boat listed decidedly to one side. This gave me the jitters. But more importantly, I couldn't see! As I stretched on my tip toes, I reminded God (just in case He forgot), "I can't see them. Let me see them to give You glory."

But all was not lost. I had an idea! Port side was as empty as an abandoned parking lot. "God," I prayed, "bring them over to this side." Again, I had a sense of anticipation, so I moved slowly toward the side rail and stood like a lone rider waiting for the city bus. I did not have to wait long, though. Suddenly, the two humpbacks broke water right in front of me and an avalanche of spectators shifted port side to watch. Of course, this tipped the boat the other way. But I soon forgot my uneasiness.

The two fifty-footers began to roll over like huge puppy dogs, sunning their big black bellies in the bright afternoon sun. They kept on rolling, too, sometimes onto their sides so they could stretch fifteen-foot fins heavenward and then slam them repeatedly against rolling mounds of ocean. All of this as if on cue: up together, down together. Hey, was this the Fin Follies? Over again, belly up, both fins up and down, white wings flapping like sea gulls, then onto their sides, seemingly applauding the God who made them.

Again, I heard the guide exclaim, "We don't really know why whales do these behaviors."

The whales continued slamming and slapping for quite a while; their pounding seeming purposeful, almost ruthless, full of power and relentless energy.

"Boy, this is unusual to see this kind of behavior go on for so long," the guide added. Other veteran watchers agreed. It was nothing like anything they had seen before.

For those of you who are watching this video in your mind: What do you think? Is it too much to imagine that the Creator of the heavens and the earth would answer a prayer like mine?

Listen to what the prophet Daniel has to say about it.

> *"O ye whales, and all that move in the waters, bless the Lord: praise and exalt him above all forever."* Daniel 3:79 DRA

Somewhere in that big ocean a mighty whale is doing this very thing.

True Devotion to the Rosary

Joe Gering

On January 5, 2011, I got a call from the nursing home that my father had just died. I immediately left a luncheon on the other side of town, and arrived at my destination in about thirty minutes. As I got off the elevator on Dad's floor, one of the nurses met me and said, "I am so sorry. Your father <u>did</u> die," she stuttered. "He was dead for several minutes. However, now he is alive and awake in his bed!"

As I walked into his room, Dad said, "Oh Joe, am I glad to see you. I've got to go to the bathroom!" While I was helping Dad in the bathroom, another nurse came in and almost passed out when she saw this man, who was dead less than an hour before, alive and standing in the bathroom.

Fr. Al came that night to the nursing home and administered the last rights to my father.

Dad was always praying the rosary. Our Blessed Mother Mary made fifteen promises to those who pray the rosary. Promise number seven is: "Whoever shall have a true devotion for the Rosary shall not die without the sacraments of the Church."

Jesus and Mary kept their promise. Dad died fifteen days later.

"Those who honor your name trust in You; You never forsake those who seek you, Lord."
Psalm 9:11

Adoration Substitute

Claire Patterson

I was praying in an Adoration[1] Chapel inside a large retreat center. I had a doctor's appointment that could not be rescheduled, so I needed to leave the chapel fifteen minutes earlier than my scheduled hour of Adoration. While exiting the chapel, I prayed that Jesus would not be left alone for long.

After taking a few steps into the hallway, I encountered a woman I did not know. She said, "Excuse me. I was told there is an Adoration Chapel in this building. Do you know where it is?" I gladly showed her the way, thanking God with each step for answering my prayer.

"Adoration of the Blessed Sacrament is the best time you will spend on earth…A Holy Hour of Adoration helps bring everlasting peace to your soul and in your family…If you are busy, spend an hour in adoration. If you are very, very busy, spend two."
St. Mother Theresa of Calcutta

An Elusive Contact Lens

Anonymous

My uncle, a thoracic surgeon, was a devout Catholic. He was generous with his time and resources in building up his local parish and helping others grow closer to God.

At one of our family's gatherings, he shared this story with me:

He and his surgical team were performing a routine abdominal surgery on a woman, when suddenly one of the operating room nurses gasped. A contact lens had just popped off her eye and landed into the surgical site! (This was back in the day when contact lenses were a novelty item.)

My uncle, the Doctor, searched diligently for the hard, clear plastic disc "for what seemed like an hour" to no avail. He could not just leave it there. He was in a quandary.

Everyone in the room was concerned and a little panicky.

Eventually, he stepped back, took a deep breath and told the surgical team to "Take time out to pray." Their prayer together was sincere and from the heart.

Upon searching again, after prayer, he immediately found that elusive little contact lens!

"Do not let your hearts be troubled. You have
faith in God; have faith also in Me."
John 14:1

Miracle From Our Lady's Farm

Lori Taylor

On January 11th, 2021, I had surgery to remove a football-sized tumor from my uterus. We prayed that it wasn't cancer; but we learned it was Leiomyosarcoma cancer. This type of cancer is aggressive and very resistant to chemotherapy and radiation treatment. I was told there was an eighty percent chance of the cancer coming back within the next two years; so, if there was anything in life I would regret not doing before death, I should do it quickly.

I decided to undergo twelve sessions of chemotherapy treatment. I was scheduled to scan for cancer every three months thereafter.

I was no longer practicing my faith as I should. My faith in God never wavered, but I felt I was not being faithful to Jesus Christ as He deserved. Friends surrounded me with prayers during this time, and my husband and I grew stronger in our faith. We went back to Sunday Mass and saying daily prayers.

But a scan on November 15th, showed the cancer had come back. This time it was inoperable. The tumor was located on my left ureter. My local cancer team recommended trying radiation, since my earlier chemotherapy had been ineffective. So, on December 1, I started a five-week daily radiation program covering my entire pelvic area.

Meanwhile, a friend, to whom I will remain forever grateful, told me about her experience at Our Lady's Farm[20] in Falmouth, Kentucky; about the miracles that had happened there, and the peace it brings to many. On December 8th, the Feast of the Immaculate Conception, I traveled there with my parents. A friend introduced us to Jerry McLafferty, who filled us in on the history of The Farm.

Before we left, Jerry, and at least fifteen other people, including my parents, prayed over me at the altar and at the foot of the cross. It was an amazing day that inspired so much hope and peace to me and my family.

My oncologist recommended that we scan again two and a half weeks into my five-week radiation program to see if the tumor was shrinking. On Friday, December 17th my 9:00 a.m. scan showed that the tumor had doubled in size. With that news came the recommendation that we abandon radiation. It was evidently not working, and the only thing left to try was chemotherapy again. After a few hours of shared tears, my husband asked, "What do you want to do?" I replied, "Can we go to Our Lady's Farm? I want to get the healing water from there and pray." We went back and found Jerry McLafferty again.

I reminded Jerry who I was and that I had just received terrible news. He invited us into the chapel. He prayed with us and I informed him that the only reason I may have to pause in praying is if I get a call from my oncologist. When the call came, Jerry suggested that I take the call at the foot of the cross. I knelt below Jesus Christ, looking up at his face, and heard only the same ideas that were mentioned during the afternoon call.

My mind was racing and I only remember praying, "Please Jesus, could I finish my radiation program and avoid chemotherapy?"

When we finished praying, my daughter called and begged me to call Dana Farber Cancer Institute in Boston. She had been following a Facebook website on my disease and read that several people had gotten good results from that clinic.

My daughter called my brother-in-law, a retired CEO of a hospital in Illinois. She asked Uncle Kevin to try to get me admitted into the Dana Farber Institute immediately. Two days later I received a call from an oncologist at Dana Farber Cancer Institute, who asked me to send all of my medical records. Since we were getting so close to the holidays, the only time she could meet me was in two days!

My husband and I booked a flight to Boston immediately and met her at 1:30 p.m. on Tuesday, Dec 21. The oncologist and a surgeon had reviewed my records. They told me that they couldn't cure me, but that he could remove the tumor and give me time to live. We were all for that. They also wanted me to finish my radiation program, give my body a rest for four weeks, and follow up with surgery in February. I asked if I would have to undergo chemotherapy after surgery. They both said "No!". My prayers to avoid chemotherapy were being answered.

On February 7th, 2022, I underwent a seven-hour surgery. It went well. My surgeon told us that it was possible that this might not be metastatic; there was at least a chance that I would be cured. We were thrilled.

I spent seven days recuperating at the hospital in Boston. On the sixth day, they told me I was doing well and that I HAD to go home the next day. I wasn't ready to go home with tubes and a catheter still connected to my body. My one drain, in particular, always filled up quickly with fluid; besides, they had said it could take two weeks before it would stop draining. Tears began to flow; I didn't feel well enough to leave the hospital.

My husband tried to calm me and suggested we pray. It was 3:00 p.m. and we prayed the Chaplet of Divine Mercy[3]. Six hours later the nurse came in to drain my tube. It was empty. The nurse was shocked, saying she had no explanation, but said if it continued to stay empty, this tube could come out the next day before I was released for home. My husband and I were speechless, and knew we were experiencing the power of God.

My husband asked me, "Do you know what I prayed for? I prayed to God, 'Please show me that your miracle is complete and that my wife is truly cured!'"

The tube came out the next day and I went home. I had some minor complications, but nothing worrisome. I was scanned every three months and had three cancer-free scans following surgery. Every time I got scared, I remembered my husband's prayers in the hospital.

I appreciate that I was given those miraculous signs. They gave me so much to cling to every three months and ease the anxiety of scanning.

These experiences definitely demonstrated the power of prayer. Thanks to my family and friends, there were literally thousands of people praying for me! I was on prayer chains across the country. It was incredible!

One of my prayer requests to Jesus Christ and Mary was to see my daughter get married on June 17th, 2023. I had a scan two weeks before her wedding and it was completely clear, allowing me to enjoy every minute of it worry free. And of course, it was probably the most beautiful day of the year. My daughter especially prayed for wonderful weather and her prayers were answered too. It was such an amazing gift and I am forever grateful.

During the last scan, they found more cancer, but I have been given a fighting chance this time around. This cancer is operable, and I will continue to pray. I have prayed more in the last two and a half years than I ever did before. I may have to deal with cancer now and again, but now I know it is God's will.

I know my miracle started at the foot of the cross at Our Lady's Farm, beginning on December 8th, and again on December 17th. I will be forever grateful, and want to thank God and our Blessed Mother from the bottom of my heart. I will try my best to evangelize His name with eternal gratitude for the rest of my life.

"...Thank God! Give Him the praise and the glory. Before all the living, acknowledge the many good things He has done for you, by blessing and extoling His name in song. Before all men, honor and proclaim God's deeds, and do not be slack in praising Him."

Tobit 12:6

CHAPTER 10

Gifts from Heaven

"Ask and it will be given to you; seek and you will find; knock and the door will be opened." Matthew 7:7

The Car

Anonymous

My husband was a salesman for several companies. The biggest company was not paying him any longer, as they were going out of business. We were experiencing an economic loss.

We had only one car. Well, it was not really a car; it was a truck with an extra-long cab with a back seat. It was a big one. My husband needed it to travel with all the products he sold. So, I would wait for him to come home on the weekends to care for our three small children, and then go to the grocery store.

After a particularly stressful day, I came out of the grocery store and put the bags in the back cab of the truck. I sat inside and just "told" God, through my tears, that this was not working out. "I can't drive this big thing around town, much less in parking lots, backing in and out of parking spots. The groceries get rolled all around in the back of the truck and it's not good." Then I "told" God, "I need a car! Please make it possible to have a car."

I pulled into the driveway at home and re-bagged the groceries, which had been all over the back of the truck by then, and carried them inside. The phone rang. I grabbed it, almost dropping the groceries. It was a friend of mine who said, "My dad just gave us his car and I don't want to sell ours and have strangers walking on our property to buy it. Would you take our old car for me?"

What? I thought she wanted me to buy her car. She said, "No, just take it. It's free. I'll probably have to charge you one dollar because of the license department getting the sale straight, but that should be alright. Right?"

Really, I had just told God that "I need a car," not ten minutes before she called! I told her my story, and she was so happy that she could participate in God's work!

Mary's Perfume

Suzanne Carvalho

Our Lady, the Blessed Mother, has a unique perfume that was revealed to me, by the Grace of God.

The first time was many years ago. Father Leroy Smith had formed a prayer group for the "Five First Saturdays"[8] of each month. Our group was scheduled to visit a different church each month to pray the rosary. Our first meeting was at a church in Cold Spring, KY.

In the church's parking lot, I stood in front of Mary's statue. I was brokenhearted because a month earlier, our son, Alexandre, had been murdered. I walked up close to the statue and held Mary's hands saying, "Mother, you know what it is like to have your son's friend betray him." Her perfume emanated from her tears. That was my first experience smelling that sweet essence.

Another time, when our children were students in elementary school, there was an opportunity for each family to borrow the statue of our Lady of Fatima for the weekend. After praying before her statue for three days, I was preparing for her departure. I placed her statue gently into the case, as the room filled with her heavenly perfume.

The Smell of Roses

Jenni VonLehman

It was December 8, 2011. I had been told about a special hour of prayer to honor Our Lady and her Feast of the Immaculate Conception. We were asked to pray a rosary and special prayers, wherever we were, between noon and 1:00 p.m.

My mother had been diagnosed with cancer at that time, and was nearing her final days. The youngest of my seven children was about to turn one. It was a dreary gray day, pretty cold outside, and I definitely wasn't in the mood to pray. However, I put the baby in the stroller, bundled him up, and took him for a walk at noon so that I could pray. I remember feeling stubborn. I didn't feel like participating in the holy hour, but willed myself to do it anyway.

I walked on a busy street, feeling the cold wind as the cars passed by. The air was stale. Life seemed gloomy. I prayed the rosary, and as I prayed, I began to develop a sense of tranquility. By the end of the rosary, I was experiencing the kind of peace that can only come from God. I heard in my heart that Mary was telling me everyone in my family was going to be OK, and that she loved each of us so much; more than I could ever know.

She mentioned every person in my family, starting with my mom, and including my brother, who was a fallen-away Catholic who never attended church. Yes, Mary loved him passionately and wanted me to love him just as much. I felt transformed.

What happened next was odd. I smelled roses. At first, I thought it was just a memory or my imagination, but as I continued to walk down the busy city street, the fragrance grew more intense and tended to linger, following me as I walked. I looked around to see if there were any rose bushes in bloom, but of course there weren't. We live in Northern Kentucky; plants at that time of the year are dormant. There are no flowers; just brown grass, gray skies, and leafless trees. As I continued to walk the scent was unceasing. All I should have smelled was car exhaust! I knew that God was letting me know that my mom was in Our Blessed Mother's tender loving care.

Thank you, Mother Mary! That was a wonderful gift of grace I will never forget! I'm surprised that you love me enough to send me your special messages, and I joyfully receive your gift of love.

"Peace, I leave with you; My peace I give you. Not as the world gives do I give it to you. Do not let your hearts be troubled or afraid." John 14:27

Mary at the Foot of the Cross

Claire Patterson

In 1983 I attended Good Friday evening services at my church. Duke stayed home with our children. Part of the service was a Passion Play.

A few of the parishioners, in costume, took the roles of people witnessing the passion of Jesus. I was acquainted with the woman who played Jesus' mother, but we were not friends.

At the end of the play, she was at the foot of the cross crying and praying. That was the moment the "play" became very real for me. It seemed that I was hearing our Blessed Mother crying and praying to God. I had chills and began to cry myself.

After the "performance", I approached the lady who had played Mary. I told her that I had heard Mary speaking through her. She looked at me very seriously and said, "She was." We were both overcome by what had just happened. We hugged and cried as we embraced. I ran home with joy and excitement. It was one of those moments I will never forget.

"Into Your hands I commend my Spirit; You will redeem me Lord, faithful God" Psalm 31:6

"Jesus cried out in a loud voice, 'Father, into Your hands, I commend My Spirit'; and when He had said this, He breathed His last." Luke 23:46

Clothes for a Needy Boy

Joe Gering

One day in the summer of 2017, I had spent the day at an amusement park with my daughter and grandson. We were in the parking lot getting ready to leave, when we ran into a friend we hadn't seen for a couple of years.

As we were talking to this lady, she told us she was planning to send her son to a Catholic school that year, but was having difficulty finding school uniforms for him. Money was tight for her.

My daughter happened to have several bags of clothes in the trunk of my car that her son had outgrown. We were planning to drop the bags off at a Goodwill location on our way home. We offered the bags of clothes to our friend, who discovered it was exactly what she needed for her son – school uniforms and all!

Some would say it was coincidence; I would say it was Divine Providence.

A Rare Gift

Claire Patterson

In May 1999, my husband, Duke, and I took a short trip to Michigan with his parents and their friends, Jeannie and Marvin. I discovered, during that trip, that this special couple had traveled to Medjugorje[11] a few years earlier. I was very excited to talk to them about their experiences.

Jeannie told me several things that had happened to her and Marvin, during their trip to this small Croatian town in 1994.

One time, the video camera they had taken got wet from the rain. It should have been inoperable after such a soaking, but it still worked and saved everything they wanted it to record.

Another time, Jeannie, who was in her sixties and experiencing heart trouble, was not able to climb Apparition Hill[2] with the others. She sat on a low wall at the foot of the hill crying, because she regretted missing this wonderful experience. A nice young man saw her and sat with her. He comforted her until her husband and the rest of their party came back down the hill. One member of the party recognized the young man as Ivan Dragicevic, one of the visionaries of Medjugorje.

So, Jeannie had received a rare gift from God that very few pilgrims ever experience!

Tuition

Anonymous

Our three children were attending a Catholic school in Cincinnati that was expensive for our family. We lived across the river in Kentucky, but the school was within driving distance from our home. One mother, with a student in the same school, saw an article in the newspaper about help with tuition for schools in Cincinnati. She cut it out and distributed it to the families at the school. I thought, "What the heck, I'll give it a try," having no idea what to expect.

A few weeks later, I received a call from a man wanting to speak to me about tuition. When he first began talking, I thought he was trying to sell me something. I was going to hang up when he shouted at me <u>not</u> to hang up. He told me that our family had won the drawing! He continued, explaining to me that I needed to attend a meeting in that city to find out just how much help with tuition we would be given.

I went to the meeting with my kids in tow. It was amazing! Such a gift! They would pay 75% of the tuition for our three children for four years. Yes, FOUR years!!! After one year, our oldest son entered the Apostolic School in New Hampshire, far from home, to discern his vocation to be a priest with the Legionaries of Christ. I called the man to let him know that our son would not be going to the school in Cincinnati any longer, and would be out of state. The man asked a lot of questions about where our son was going and why. He said they might still be able to help. After a week he called me back. He said they would continue the grant as promised at 75% of the tuition for the school in Cincinnati for our two children, AND for our son in the school in New Hampshire.

I called the man again when my husband had gotten a much better job, and offered to give this scholarship to another family more needy than we were. But he said, "No. You were given this gift, and it is for four years. Keep it." So, we did.

Our second son then left the school in Cincinnati to go to the Apostolic School in New Hampshire with his brother. I called the man again and he said the tuition aid was still good. Again, he said, "Keep it."

After this scholarship ran out, we were back to paying full tuition for high school for our daughter and the school in New Hampshire for our two older sons. It got costly.

My husband was on a committee for our parish retreats with another parishioner. That man had three brothers who were priests and three sisters who were consecrated religious. He had heard about our two sons attending the school in New Hampshire. He said, "I hear that you have two sons discerning the priesthood. That must be expensive for room, board and tuition for both." My husband answered, "Yes." The man then asked how much it was costing us for tuition, room and board, etc. My husband told him the amount. The man then said to my husband, "How about if I pay for one and you pay for the other?" Wow! Such a generous man! He did, too. He kept that promise until they graduated. Our two sons are now priests! God must have really wanted our sons to become priests, as He clearly paved the way!

"It is a Plenary Indulgence!"

Peggy B.

"Lord, I believe in Thee: may I believe more strongly. I trust in Thee: may I hope more confidently." Pope Clement XI

In October 2015, my mother was in hospice and in her final days. When I got the notice that she had slipped into a coma, I made the long journey from Northern Kentucky to just south of Chicago, Illinois. I went straight to the nursing care facility to be with her. While I was there, a minister of a different faith came in to pray with me. After he left, I tried to contact a priest to administer the Last Rites to Mom.

Time was imminent. I called my sister who lived nearby and she had told me that hospice would probably take care of finding a priest for us. Not satisfied with that answer, I visited my old parish where I had grown up, and was informed that ALL the priests in the diocese were attending a convocation at that time, and no one was available until the following day.

I sat in the parking lot outside the parish office crying. It suddenly occurred to me to call my mother's current parish, only three miles away, just to inquire about the availability of a priest. As I was speaking to the parish secretary, a volunteer in the office overheard her mention my mother's name and got on the phone with me. She knew my mother from the women's group. I explained the situation, and she informed me that there was a retired priest whom she chauffeurs around to his various appointments. She took my phone number and said to wait until she contacted him. Within five minutes, this kind lady called me back and told me that she would pick up Father, bring him to the nursing home, and meet us there.

I was ecstatic with joy! I quickly called my sister, and told her to come. As I was waiting in the reception area for the priest to arrive, my brother, also a local resident, walked in. A few minutes later, my nephew came in through the door. Soon, the helpful volunteer arrived with the priest.

After assisting him with his walker, and balancing his prayer book and the vial of oil on the seat, we led Father through the many wheelchairs in the hallway to my mother's room.

Father gently anointed my mother with the holy oil and then said in a loud voice: "Go be with God, Catherine! It's a plenary indulgence![21]"

My joy overflowed, as this was the last gift I could give to my mother. She went home to be with God at 8:55 a.m. the following morning with her children by her side. God is good all the time!

"Lord, I adore Thee as my first beginning. I long for Thee as my last end. I praise Thee as my constant benefactor. I invoke Thee as my gracious protector."
Pope Clement XI

An Appendicitis Blessing

Janet H.

I am well past retirement age, and some would refer to me as an "elderly woman."

About two years ago, during the COVID pandemic, I experienced sharp abdominal pains on my right side. The pains continued, so my husband and I went to the hospital emergency room. A short time later, my suspicions were confirmed; I had appendicitis!

Surgery was scheduled for later that night. The doctor spoke reassuringly about the surgical procedure, but I told him that I had already put myself in the Lord's hands and that I would also put myself in the doctor's hands. The surgery was successful, and I went home the next day.

At the post-op appointment the following week, the doctor showed me the biopsy report. To my surprise, he said that they had found a fast-growing pre-cancerous polyp in the appendix, and that it would not have been detected by a colonoscopy or a CT scan. The only way it could have been found was through the appendicitis procedure I had just experienced!

This was a great blessing! I thanked God and continue to thank God for giving me appendicitis at that critical time, when it was the only way to detect the polyp, and to eliminate the more serious disease.

Thanks be to God! His love is Everlasting!

The Miraculous Medal

Claire Patterson

In the summer of 2001, I was given Three Miraculous Medals[13] during confession in Medjugorje[11]. The priest told me that they had been blessed by the Virgin Mary on Apparition Hill[2] the evening before my visit, and he had also blessed them. I treasured those tiny tin medals above all of my possessions. No gold or jewels could ever compare.

I put one on the chain around my neck immediately and gave one to my husband as soon as I met him after my confession. I gave the third medal, a few weeks later, to a stranger. She has since become a dear friend.

For a long time, I kept the medal on a chain around my neck. When the loop of metal, through which the chain was threaded broke off, I pinned the medal to my bra. I wore it all day, every day. Then it was suggested to me to pin it to my scapular,[22] so that I could also wear it while I slept. Over time, my scapulars wore out and were replaced, but I always pinned the Miraculous Medal to the current one.

When I fell in 2023, I fractured my back. As they removed my clothing in the hospital, I kept my scapular on under my hospital gown. When they wheeled me into surgery, I asked permission to put my scapular and medal into the pocket of my gown. They were fine with it.

After waking up following surgery, I took the scapular out of my pocket, with the Miraculous Medal still attached by a safety pin, and looped it over my head. I tucked it under my gown, and thought no more about it.

The next morning, two nurses came into my room and asked me to roll onto my stomach so they could check the incision. One of them said, "What is that?" I said, "It's just my scapular." She said, "No. It's a small piece of metal. It's stuck to your back." I got a bit concerned. I couldn't imagine what they were talking about. I began thinking, "Did they insert a rod or screw into my back and forget to tell me? Is it now protruding from my skin?"

As I lay face-down, one of the nurses peeled the object off my back, as it had been stuck to the iodine smeared over surgical area. I was still lying on my stomach, so she brought it into my view with her finger. It was a piece of my Miraculous Medal. One small piece is still missing, along with the safety pin, but she had found the main part of the medal. With a sigh of relief, I told them, "The scapular can be replaced easily; the medal – not so much. Thank you." She put it carefully into my glasses case for safekeeping.

I didn't think about that incident until a week later. Many people who break their backs become paralyzed or live with pain for the rest of their lives. My prognosis could have been so much worse! Modern science has invented a simple way to fix a fractured vertebra (at least in my case) and I was fortunate to experience a procedure during which they injected medical "cement" to mend my bones. Thanks be to God, I have made a quick recovery.

Was I just lucky? I don't think so. I believe Our Blessed Mother and her precious Son, Jesus, had a plan for that medal all along. It's not called the "Miraculous Medal" for nothing!

"Put it into your heart, my youngest and dearest son, that the thing that disturbs you, the thing that afflicts you, is nothing. Do not let your heart be troubled. Do not fear this or any other thing. Am I not here, I who am your Mother? Are you not under my protection? Am I not the source of your joy? Are you not in the hollow of my mantle, in the crossing of my arms? Do you need anything more? Let nothing else worry or disturb you."

Our Lady of Guadalupe[17] to St. Juan Diego

Escanaba, Apple Pie, and Pepper

Barbara C. DeNamur

In 1975 my husband, Ron, and I were moving to Green Bay, Wisconsin where he had been assigned to engineer the design controls for the new Posh Puffs line. We traveled through Michigan to see our families along the way.

As we were driving in the Upper Peninsula, we drove through many small towns. About five miles past Escanaba, a rock flew up and hit the radiator of Ron's 1969 Buick. Steam poured out and shot straight up. Ron brought the car to a stop on a sandy side road next to the highway. When he raised the hood on the engine, Ron said, "It looks like we'll have to walk back to town."

It was after 5:00 p.m. on a Friday night. Just as I was looking for my tennis shoes for the long hike ahead, a man stopped his car and got out to see what we needed. He had a strong rope with him and offered to tow our car back to Escanaba. He was driving a station wagon full of kids in bathing suits. Ron stayed in our car, and I rode with the wet children and listened to their chatter. It was fun to feel like part of this happy family. I felt a peaceful joy in my heart and I thanked God for sending help at the exact time we needed it. I could not believe that we barely had time to discover our problem when this wonderful man and his children showed up to help.

When we arrived at the home of our rescuer, he called his friend who owned the radiator repair shop. The shop was closed for the night, but the owner promised to have his workmen look at the situation the next day. Ron and our new friend took our car over to the radiator shop.

I stayed behind with the rescuer's wife. As I was led into her kitchen, the heavenly smells of cinnamon and apples and spicy aromas of soup made my mouth water. This was an old-fashioned kitchen with a checkered cloth on the table and herb pots on the windowsill. I told this delightful lady what had happened on our drive and how fortunate we were to be saved by her husband. I also complimented her cooking and told her that she should bottle the scents coming from her kitchen. She laughed when I said, "It would make a popular air freshener."

She invited us to stay for supper when Ron and her husband returned. Before the meal, the family said grace and prayed for us and our safe travels. I couldn't help but think how our situation had drastically changed. We had been destined to walk five miles along a two-lane highway, and instead, we enjoyed the company of this beautiful family. It felt like a dream or a Hallmark movie. The chicken soup with homemade biscuits, followed by apple pie was a heartwarming experience in dining. We thanked the family for their hospitality, which had been beyond compare.

After dinner, they helped us find a motel down the street from the radiator repair shop. The wife even called us the next morning to ask if we needed anything else. We thanked her, for she had far exceeded our expectations. I asked for her name and address while Ron walked down to the repair shop. We were on our way by noon.

I don't know for sure, but I feel like God led our rescuer to us just at the moment we needed help. They were Good Samaritans of the best kind. Also, I discovered that their last name was Pepper, so I remember them as "the salt of the earth."

"Will You Take Me to Medjugorje?"

Claire Patterson

In the fall of 2018, I gave a talk to a church group in Indiana. I told them about the trip my husband, Duke, and I had made to Medjugorje[11], Croatia in 2001, and described all the blessings we had received since that time.

After the talk, a woman in her eighties, named Rosella, approached me and asked if I would take her to Medjugorje. The Holy Spirit encouraged me to say "Yes!" immediately. We exchanged contact information and I promised to send her some options of dates and tours.

As Rosella did not have an email address, I sent everything to her daughter. I tried to convince her daughter to go with us because I was beginning to feel uncomfortable taking a woman in her eighth decade to a somewhat primitive area. The daughter was clear with me that it was her mother's desire to go; not hers. So, I did a lot of praying.

Our pilgrimage occurred in early May 2019. During our flight from the U.S., my traveling companion showed me a newspaper clipping that she wanted to discuss with Father Leon, a priest living in Medjugorje. I was aware that he was assigned to provide orientation talks for the English-speaking pilgrims. I knew that his schedule was pretty full, and I told her that I doubted she would have a chance to talk to him privately.

On the day we decided to go to confession, there were two very long lines for English-speaking pilgrims. My new friend got in one line, and I filed into the other. We finished about the same time. I had confessed to a young priest from Ireland, and, amazingly, Rosella's confessor had been Father Leon! She had been given the opportunity to talk to him at length about the article from the newspaper, and everything else she wanted to tell him. God is good!

We were very blessed to stay at Mirjana Soldo's guest house. She is one of the six visionaries in Medjugorje, who have experienced apparitions with Our Blessed Mother since 1981. We were fortunate to spend time with her, as well as her husband and two daughters. We were also present during Mirjana's May 2, 2019 apparition at the Blue Cross. Some pilgrims had begun arriving as early as 4:30 a.m. in order to get a spot close to the visionary. They gathered on a rocky hillside.

As so many people came from all over the world for those public apparitions, Rosella and I decided not to join the crowd. We were invited to climb on top of the roof of the hostel where we were staying. We brought folding chairs and were situated on our perch by 8:00 a.m. We could see many of the approximately ten thousand pilgrims as they gathered below, and we could hear everything clearly.

Before the apparition began, music and prayers were broadcast over loud speakers. When Mary appeared to Mirjana, about 9:30 that morning, there was an announcement, "Silencio!" Everyone hushed, except for a woman wailing loudly. (This type of wailing often occurred because a possessed person's demon is afraid of Our Lady.)

About fifteen minutes later, the message Mary had given to Mirjana was read aloud in Croatian, Italian, and English. We couldn't see Mirjana from our rooftop, but neither could most of the people who were crowded below.

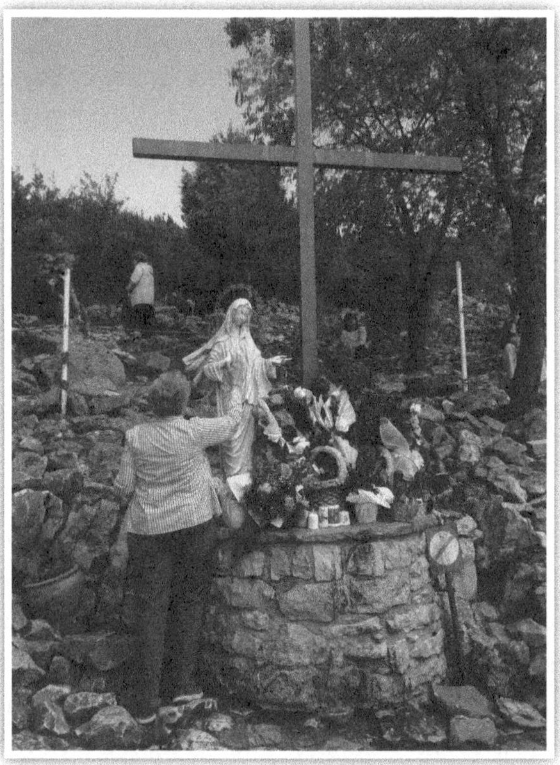

We made sure to visit the site of the Blue Cross the next day, where we could stand on the rocks and be in the place where Mary had appeared the day before. It turned out that my elderly companion had more energy than I did! She even took an optional trip one day while I stayed in our room to rest.

Holy Moments

Anonymous

My most profound holy moments have occurred during Adoration[1] and Benedictions.

The first was nearly ten years ago at a healing Mass and Benediction for cancer patients. I was attending that service when I looked up at the monstrance[14], containing the Consecrated Host, and said, "Jesus are you really here?" Then, His face appeared in the Host! I kept opening and closing and rubbing my eyes in disbelief, but each time I looked, His face was still there.

"...and the
bread
that I
will give
...is my flesh
for the life
of the world."
-John 6:52
P. Bethell 2010

Then, an enormous cloud appeared over the altar and I was transfixed.

A few weeks later, in my bible study class on the book of Exodus, I learned that the cloud was a sign of God's presence and guidance in the desert.

Several years later I was in an Adoration Chapel. I was praying for a member of my family who was going through a very difficult time. I looked up at the monstrance and saw that person's face in the Host. Again, I looked away and looked back in disbelief, but that person's face continued to appear. I prayed for him even more intently.

A third instance was years later, at another healing Mass. At this event, each person was invited to come up to the altar and touch and pray by the monstrance that the priest was holding. I looked at the Host, in very close view, and saw a vast number of human faces flashing before me; some were people I did not recognize; some I knew. Every few seconds a new face was visible. God seemed to be saying, "All people should be seen as Jesus."

Recently I read the book, The Jewish Roots of the Eucharist. It said that the "Bread of the Presence" in the Ark of the Covenant, was also called the "Bread of the Face!" Wow, that really connected with me.

The song "Jesus, my Lord, my God, my All, How can I love You as I Ought?" keeps reverberating in my head, since I recently visited the Holy Land. I pray, "How can I love YOU, God?" He answers me, "Love My Lambs!"

"Jesus said to them, 'I am the bread of life; whoever comes to Me will never hunger, and whoever believes in Me will never thirst.'" John 6:35

"Eucharistic Adoration is the greatest power in the universe, capable of transforming us and changing the face of the world."
St. Maximilian Kolbe

Our Lady of Light and St. Padre Pio

Anonymous

I went with friends a few times to St. Joseph's Church in Cold Spring, Kentucky, at the time when Our Blessed Mother Mary began appearing there in 1994. I seem to remember being inside the church on one occasion, and at other times in the crowd assembled outside. I saw flashes of lights, but I didn't notice anything particularly unusual about them. These lights were not coming from the sky; I only saw what looked to me like a lot of camera flashes, as many people in the crowd had cameras.

Some people began to whisper excitedly, "Mary's here! Mary's here!" Not knowing much about Mary's appearances throughout history, I thought that if Mary appeared, at least everyone in front of the crowd would see her. No one I was with saw Mary that night. I became somewhat skeptical about the whole thing.

Despite my growing doubts about "Our Lady of Light,"[19] as folks began to call this series of apparitions, I went to morning Mass at St. Joseph's on a certain Saturday when it was said that Mary would appear. No one I knew saw any lights or signs of Mary's presence on that Saturday.

However, something supernatural did occur that morning.

My close friends were in Church with me. Before Mass, Grace saw a person near the altar. She presumed he was a visiting priest. She asked her husband if he knew who that was in the sanctuary. Grace became frustrated because her husband didn't understand what she was asking. Mass started, and the incident was dismissed.

During the Consecration, Grace saw the "priest" step toward the altar; he was gone after Holy Communion. When Mass was over, Grace explained what she saw, insistent that we should have noticed the priest or monk on the altar. Her husband said again, that he hadn't seen any such person.

As Grace was telling us what she had seen, a woman rushed over bubbling with excitement, saying she too had seen the priest about whom she had overheard Grace talking. Both Grace and the woman described the visitor as an older man with a long gray beard, wearing a monk's garb with a dark hood. The two ladies had identical recollections of all his movements in the sanctuary, including the exact door through which he exited.

None of the rest of us had seen the monk they were describing. Grace proclaimed that the mysterious figure had to be St. Padre Pio![25] The incident astounded us and strengthened our faith.

> *"...No ear has ever heard, no eye ever seen any God but you doing such deeds for those who wait for Him." Isaiah 64:3*

CHAPTER 11

Messages from Heaven

"But we hold this treasure in earthen vessels,
that the surpassing power may be of God and not from us."
2 Corinthians 4:7

My Perpetual Vows

Anonymous

As seminarians, we renew our vows every three years. The last of the vows is called the "Perpetual Vows". These vows cannot be expunged without the Vatican dissolving them.

My vows were taken in Rome during my thirty-day retreat. If I continued in the seminary, my final vows would be for the priesthood. So, these vows were very important to me as a seminarian. A lot of the seminarians take this time during the thirty-day retreat to decide if they should keep going in the program or drop out. I had put the "Perpetual Vows" off for a couple of years because I was just not sure what God was calling me to do. This was my last chance to drop out. I needed a sign from God to stay, or not to stay.

Seminarians are told to request something of God as proof that this is the right thing to do; that this is His will. St. Therese of Lisieux[27] asked for snow on a warm day when she took her vows, and it snowed! Well, I asked for a big storm with lightning and thunder.

This was like the boat on the Sea of Galilee. The Apostles were in a terrible storm while Jesus was asleep in the boat. When Jesus calmed the storm, the apostles asked each other,

> *"...What sort of man is this? Whom even the winds and the sea obey?"* Matthew 8:27

So, I asked for a big storm.

Then on that morning, I relented. Other seminarians were praying for nice weather, sunshine and warmth because their relatives would be there, and really that's something that everyone wants. So, I just told God that He could do whatever He wanted with the weather because I didn't want it to "rain on their parade".

We all went into the church with the sun brightly shining and the warm breezes blowing. We were all kneeling on the altar, and one by one the other men were answering, "Present," as their names were called. Then, it was my turn. As soon as they started saying my name, the biggest clap of thunder and lightning seemed to shout their loudest, and buckets of rain came down for just a short while. I proudly and lovingly answered, "Present," with a big smile for God saying, "Thank You" in my heart. Everyone was looking at me, wondering what was going on.

The rain stopped shortly after our vows and for the rest of the Mass. We all walked out of the church to sunshine and warmth again! I was reassured that God wanted me as one of His Shepherds. He had given me the sign I had asked for and caused no problems for anyone else.

Pennies from Heaven

Marianne Dammert

Even after her funeral, it was hard to believe Nancy had really left our world. It had only been three months since she was diagnosed with lung cancer. We had prayed for her recovery. Why didn't God answer our prayers?

Nancy was the social worker on our rehab unit at our Hospital's Medical Center. She had a gift for communicating with even our most difficult patients and families. She helped in any way possible to make their lives better. She always had a smile on her face, a joke to brighten our day, or a wonderful story to help us put things in a proper perspective. We needed her! She was such a special part of our team. How did God think that we could ever function without her?

As we left her memorial service, a few of us didn't want to go home yet, so we met at a nearby restaurant for dinner. It felt good to be in the company of such compassionate friends, who shared such sadness. Leaving the restaurant, I spotted a shiny penny on the stairs. I told everyone I would keep it for good luck. None of us realized how significant that discovery would come to be.

The next evening at work I was assigned to April, a young woman who was dying of cancer. Our rehab unit was also designated as a hospice unit, so we occasionally had a patient whose family chose to experience the end-of-life with the support of medical staff. April never had the opportunity to meet Nancy, but her room was directly across from Nancy's office. April had seen the tributes written on Nancy's door and knew that we were grieving her illness.

When Nancy died, I felt it was important to let April know, so she could understand the somber mood of our staff. In response, she told me, "You know, God has a plan for each of us. We may not like His plan, but we have to remember that it is <u>His</u> plan and trust that He knows best." What words of wisdom coming from someone who had been through so much of her own suffering!

That evening, as I helped April to the sink to wash her hands, we heard a clinking sound. I asked her what the noise was, and she responded, "It sounded like a penny." I wasn't carrying any money and neither was she, so both of us were surprised to see a penny lying at her feet. I then told her about finding a penny after Nancy's funeral, and we both laughed at the thought of Nancy throwing a penny to us from heaven.

As the days passed, I kept finding pennies in odd places, always at times when I was feeling sad or frustrated. I shared my experience with some co-workers and soon the same thing started happening to them! It was amazing how the pennies would lighten our spirits and give us the feeling that Nancy was watching over us.

One of the pennies actually came in a different form after my friend, Debbie, had a difficult evening. She was wishing she would find a penny to comfort her when her patient had a change in his status and had to be transferred to the Intensive Care Unit. There were no pennies in his room, our medication room or the hallways as others had found. Imagine her surprise when the nurse who arrived to help with the transport introduced herself as "Penny"!

Not long after that event, I was surprised to find an e-mail from my nephew, Lee, from New York. As part of his message, he included a poem entitled "Pennies from Heaven" by Charles Mashburn. (It is copied here with permission from Mr. Mashburn.)

I found a penny today
Just lying on the ground.
But it's not just a penny,
This little coin I found.

Found pennies come from heaven.
That's what my Grandpa told me.
He said angels toss them down.
Oh, how I love that story.

He said when an angel misses you,
They toss a penny down.
Sometimes just to cheer you up,
To make a smile out of your frown.

So don't pass by that penny
When you are feeling blue.
It may be a penny from heaven
That an angel tossed to you.

I cried as I read those words. Lee had no idea what we had just experienced with Nancy's death and the finding of the pennies. I shared the poem with my friends and coworkers the next day.

Later that month, I was at a church meeting where we shared everyday examples of how we bring Christ into our family's lives. A discussion came up about our trust in God and one of the women held up a penny. She pointed out that every bit of our United States currency has the words, "IN GOD WE TRUST" imprinted on them. A chill came over me as I discovered the true meaning of our found pennies.

It was so hard to understand why Nancy died. Shortly afterwards, April followed in her path. Hospitals are full of families whose lives have been shattered by illness and accidents. We often hear the question, "Why did God let this happen?" We will probably never have an answer to take away the pain of grief, but we must learn to trust God in all circumstances. As April said, "We may not always like His plan, but it is His plan, not ours." I often share this verse from the Bible:

"We know that all things work for good for those who love God, who are called according to His purpose." Romans 8:28

This seems much better than merely telling someone, "Things happen for a reason." We know God always keeps His promises to us. Even in our grief and challenges, He is with us and for us. Our unit found comfort in our conversations about Nancy and our beliefs in where she will spend eternity.

Life goes on, and it is up to us to keep our hearts open to the people that God brings into our lives. It is so important to show our appreciation, and to love each other while we are here on earth. Even a simple smile can mean so much.

A new family lounge was opened and dedicated to the memory of Nancy. On one wall is a frame with a picture of Nancy, her business card, her signature, the penny poem and a penny with the year of her death. With a close inspection, anyone can see the words printed on that penny, "IN GOD WE TRUST."

I don't find many pennies anymore, but that's okay. I have enough "cents" to trust in God in all circumstances. He is with us always.

Lost and Found

Pat Bethell

One Friday morning, as I made coffee, I noticed the date was June 11th. That date seemed like an anniversary or special date of some sort. While pouring a cup of coffee, I noticed the "Sacred Heart of Jesus Chaplet" prayer beads hanging from the crucifix my mother had given me before she passed away. The final prayer to Jesus from this novena is a favorite of mine: "...Have pity on us miserable sinners and grant us the grace which we ask of Thee, through the Sorrowful and Immaculate Heart of Mary, Your and our, tender Mother..."

I picked up the prayer beads for the chaplet and started my morning prayers. After a while, I glanced at the calendar once again, and finally remembered why that date had haunted my memory.

I was privileged to be able to take care of my mom, my best friend, before she passed from this earth. She was a convert from the Methodist faith. As a matter of fact, her relatives started the Methodist Church in Warsaw, Kentucky. Her dad was a dairy farmer who was injured in a farm accident. As he lay on his death bed, to everyone's surprise, he asked for a priest. Granddaddy died a Catholic, changing the trajectory of our family's faith. Mom attended Mount St. Joseph College and took instructions to become a Catholic. Her faith took her through the many devotions and traditions of the Church, including the rosary. Mom and Dad had eight children who were all blessed with the Catholic faith as well.

Before Mom contracted ALS, she was active in promoting the St. Agnes Adoration Chapel[1]. She and I signed up for the 9:00 a.m. hour on Fridays, which I still honor every week.

One Friday morning, before it was time for our Holy Hour, I decided to take an early morning walk. As I came up my street to the intersection, directly across from our church, I noticed within my peripheral vision, a white piece of paper. As I kept walking, it occurred to me that I might have just passed a holy card. Turning around, I retrieved it and discovered that it was a "Novena of Confidence to the Sacred Heart." I put it in my pocket and went to pick up my mom. When we arrived at the chapel, Father Lauer's book, One Bread, One Body, which featured daily readings from the Church calendar, was lying in the pew. I looked up that day's date, June[11th]. It was the Feast of the Sacred Heart! God was certainly trying to tell me something!

Even now, many years later, fortified by the Sacred Heart Novena, coffee and early morning prayers, I make my trek to the Adoration Chapel for my weekly visit with the King of Kings and the Lord of Lords, followed by Holy Mass. Praise God!

"My soul, be at rest in God alone, from whom comes my hope. God alone is my rock and my salvation, my secure height; I shall not fall." Psalm 62:6-7

"I Have Loved You with an Everlasting Love"

Claire Patterson

My husband died in 2012. On our wedding anniversary, July 14, 2018, my daughter, Alicia, called me and said, "Mom, listen." She was on her front porch and held up her phone. I could hear the bells from a near-by church playing, "I Have Loved You with an Everlasting Love." My daughter said, "Mom, I think Daddy is sending you this song for your anniversary." Of course, we both cried tears of joy and sorrow.

On June 14, 2023, I was in the hospital, awaiting back surgery. My daughter was keeping me company and had brought her bible and daily devotional along with her. That day would have been my husband's seventy-third birthday, and often, on that special date, he sends us some kind of message to let us know he is near. I had actually said to Alicia a week before, "I wonder what kind of gift your daddy will send us on his birthday this year."

Alicia opened her daily devotional to June 14, and the first words she read were, "I have loved you with an everlasting love." Of course, tears began to flow again. God is so good to us! He provides us these messages when we most need them!

"The Lord appeared to us in the past, saying: 'I have loved you with an everlasting love; I have drawn you with unfailing kindness.'" Jeremiah 31:3 (NIV)

O Death, Where is Thy Sting?

Anonymous

Night shift nurses had just finished giving their report to us day shift nurses on the Hospice Unit. I was a little late out of the gate getting to see my patients. One of them, I was told, was on the verge of dying. The family had been notified, but they had not yet arrived, and we were informed that she remained comfortable in a non-awake state. I checked on my other patients first.

As I was walking down the hall to assess her medical status, to be sure she was still in no distress, a young man came out of her room. I guessed he was her son. I expected him to be unhappy that no staff member was with her at this critical time in her life.

He told me with a serene, almost joyous countenance, "Mom has just passed away." I could tell by his reaction that he was a deeply committed Christian who was happy for her to be at peace in the arms of God, after all the suffering she had endured was completed.

"...O Death where is thy victory? O Death, where is thy sting?"
1 Corinthians 15:55 (NASB)

"Was she a good mother?" I asked. He gazed intently into my eyes and after some thought, and with great conviction, he answered, "Oh yes, she was the best! The most important thing she taught us was: **Always forgive immediately**, no matter what the offense. And **never, ever hold a grudge**."

I was not prepared for the response he gave me. A feeling of peace enveloping these words hit me like an arrow straight through my heart. It is a moment forever frozen in my memory, when the Holy Spirit spoke special words to me – specifically for me!

I try to live by these words. I thank God for them.

This message proved to me that the secret to a life-well-lived is the holiness gained by offering forgiveness – God's Will in action – His Mercy. This beautiful soul, through her son, passed this sacred treasure on to me.

"If you forgive others their transgressions, your heavenly Father will forgive you."
Matthew 6:14

"On This Day, Oh Beautiful Mother"

Ann H.

My maternal grandmother passed away early in February, 1998. She had developed a deep devotion to the Sacred Heart of Jesus and the Immaculate Heart of Mary. I have many treasured childhood memories of her singing Marian hymns as she performed daily tasks around the house. One of her favorite songs was, "On This Day, Oh Beautiful Mother."

Two weeks after her death, I was in church remembering her prayer life and her devotions to Jesus and Mary, so I just thought to ask my grandmother if she was all right and at peace.

Now, remember, this incident took place in February. Typically, Marian hymns are not sung during that month; so, imagine my surprise when the priest, who was about to say Mass, told us, "We will begin our celebration with, 'On This Day, Oh Beautiful Mother.'"

"The Mighty One has done great things for me, and Holy is His name. His mercy is from age to age to those who fear Him. He has shown might with His arm, dispersed the arrogant of mind and heart. He has thrown down the rulers from their thrones and lifted up the lowly. The hungry He has filled with good things; the rich He has sent away empty." Luke 1:49-53

A Message from Mom

Claire Patterson

On July 9, 2001, Duke and I had climbed Apparition Hill[2] in Medjugorje[11] at 8:30 p.m. It was getting dark and we had only our flashlights to illuminate the path. (There were no electric lights on the hill then, as there are now.)

We were among ten thousand pilgrims from across the world for Ivan Dragicevic's Monday night visit with Mary. The apparition was expected to take place at approximately 10:00 p.m.

One of the remarkable things about that night was that all of those people, who were total strangers, helped one another over the large sharp rocks. There was a chain of strong arms helping pilgrims to safely navigate the steep incline. We all spoke different languages, so not many people bothered to say, "Take my hand." We climbed the hill silently. No one complained about the crowd, the discomfort, or the darkness.

Everyone on the hillside was either perched on a flat rock or standing unsteadily among jagged rocks. I was too excited to sit down. I wanted to see and hear everything! Some men were playing guitars and singing in Italian near Ivan. When the music stopped, everyone was silent, for we knew that Mary was with us.

We had been told, earlier that day, that on the next morning we would have an opportunity to hear Ivan speak. He was expected to tell us whatever the Blessed Virgin revealed to him during the apparition. So, on that hillside, I prayed the prayer of a child; "Blessed Mother, please give Ivan a message from my mother. I want to know if she is in heaven. I want to know how my mother is. I want to know if my mother is aware of my life now. Is she pleased with me?"

During the apparition, Duke saw sparks in the trees. Later, we learned that our spiritual advisor, Father Bill, had also witnessed the same sign of Mary's presence. No one else in our small group saw the sparks.

The next morning, I was anxious to find out if Ivan had been given a message for me. The lecture hall was crowded with over three hundred people, as all English-speaking pilgrims had been invited. Ivan shared the message Mary had given him the night before through an interpreter.

I kept waiting for him to say, "Is there a woman here named, Claire? I have a message for you about your mother." That is actually what I was expecting to hear him say! How silly I was, to believe that out of ten thousand people on that hill the night before, Mary would have a message especially for me. I didn't share my prayer or disappointment with anyone, not even my husband.

After we were home a few days, Duke took me outside to our deck. He held both of my hands between both of his hands (to steady me, I suppose) and said, "I have a message for you from your mother. The message is: 'Tell my Bridgie that I am in heaven, but I did spend some time in Purgatory...'" There was much more to the message, but most of it would not make sense to anyone but me. Much of it didn't even make sense to my husband, as he had never heard my mom call me, "Bridgie". That was a special name she had used when I was three or four years old. Duke had several other questions about the message, that I had to explain to him. I had to ask my brother, Tom, about a part of the message that even I didn't understand; but he did.

That spiritual experience was certainly a validation to both Duke and me that Mary was truly appearing and talking to him, and that so many other similar things that had been happening to him since July 3, 2001, were, in fact, real. (Read Finding Grace Through Mary's Eyes for more information.)

We had both been questioning: "Are these messages from Mary? Are they from Satan? Are they simply dreams?" But there were too many incidences, such as this one, that made it clear to us that Duke wasn't fabricating anything. How could he? Why would he?

After all, we gained nothing financially from Duke's claims to have received messages from Mary and Jesus, nor from his claims to have been given glimpses of Mary's life. On the contrary; visiting prayer groups and churches to share the messages, sending the messages through emails, duplicating pages of materials, maintaining a website, and self-publishing books were all done at our own expense. Furthermore, in doing all that Mary asked of us, we were frequently under attack from Satan. Worse yet, Duke suffered physically and emotionally from carrying out the tasks Mary asked of him.

"Three times I begged the Lord about this, that it (the thorn) might leave me, but he said to me, 'My Grace is sufficient for you, for power is made perfect in weakness...'"
2 Corinthians 12:8-9

Among the many blessings we did receive, were access to the fountain of God's love and grace, and the protection of His angels and saints. Our lives were much richer with God's gifts, rather than with the things of this earth.

And, yes, Mom said she is pleased with me!

Jesus Loves the Little Children

Jenni VonLehman

Around 1993, I was a stay-at-home mom with four little children. I was grappling with feelings of isolation, but I was also learning to embrace my newly rediscovered Catholic faith. Now that I look back, I see that Mary and Jesus had been seeking me and would not let me go. I am grateful that they continued their pursuit of me despite my rebuffs.

One day, as I experienced the usual daily frustrations, I took my children outside to play. I noticed the beautiful roses in our yard, and the thought occurred to me that I should bring some of these roses to Mother Mary. I had been told that she loves it when children come to visit her Son, so I announced to the kids that we were going to get in the car and take a little trip to our parish's Perpetual Adoration Chapel[1]. The weather was relatively nice as we left the house. .

When we arrived, we walked into the chapel with our roses. After we blessed ourselves with holy water and genuflected, I told the kids to kneel in the pew, and I explained that they could talk to Jesus and His holy mother, Mary. I assured them that we wouldn't stay long. I remember the children being fidgety, as I loudly whispered things like, "Stop touching your brother," "Keep your hands to yourself," and "Scooch over."

Once we were settled, I decided to ignore the kids and take advantage of my time in the chapel. I spoke to Jesus. It was one of those intimate prayers of speaking directly and honestly to God. Perhaps it was a prayer of desperation. I was tired of my husband working so many hours; tired of battling fatigue, restlessness, and selfishness. I longed for more help, more friends, more days of freedom…things I had taken for granted before embracing my new state of life as a stay-at-home mom.

I told Jesus that I really loved Him despite the fact that I was a mess and my family was a mess. I asked Him to accept my meager prayer, simply because I had nothing more to offer! I also requested His help to be a better wife and mother, and be more loving and patient. I apologized for all my failures. I brought to Him my deep struggles with disappointment, irritation, discouragement, guilt, and inadequacy.

After unloading all of my worries, I felt a little better. This was not the method of prayer I had been taught, and though it seemed disordered, it also felt right, because it was personal and honest. It was a surrender of my will to His holy and good will. (At the time I didn't realize God loves us even more when we are humble; when we are aware of our weakness, and when we draw on His Grace for our strength.)

I placed the roses under our chapel's statue of Mary holding Baby Jesus. With tears in my eyes, I told Mary that these roses were from my yard (although I knew she knew). I specifically remember telling her that I really hoped she would be PLEASED with what little we had to offer her: the humble effort to visit, the prayers, and the roses. After a few final minutes, my children and I said goodbye, genuflected again, and departed the chapel.

When we opened the doors to the outside, it was raining pretty hard, but we managed to make the short walk from the chapel to our van. There had been another gentleman in the chapel while we were there, but I hadn't paid much attention to him at the time. I don't believe I had ever seen him before. Once we were in the van, I noticed that he had followed us outside. He was a very small, humble-looking older gentleman. He waved to me as he stood in the rain. I waved back and started to leave my parking spot, but he continued moving his arm until I realized he was asking me to roll down the window.

When I did so, the man said he wanted to tell me something important. He proceeded to explain that Jesus knew I had been there in that chapel, and that He was very happy we had come to see Him. The man told me that Mary, too, was happy to see us, and loved that the children had come to visit her and her Son. The man said that Mary wanted to thank me for the roses. The last thing the man relayed to me was the most profound proclamation: Mary wanted me to know that she was PLEASED.

> *"But Jesus said, 'Let the children come to me, and do not prevent them; for the kingdom of heaven belongs to such as these.'"* Matthew 19:14

I've never seen that man again, but I'm so grateful for his response to the promptings he had received from the Holy Spirit, compelling him to deliver that astounding message from Jesus and Mary. The St. Agnes Divine Mercy Perpetual Adoration Chapel holds a very special place in my heart because of that very intimate encounter with Christ and His Mother. Since then, I continue to visit there on a regular basis. This holy place, this "sacred ground," has strengthened my relationships with Jesus and Mary throughout the years; I always feel so at home when I'm there. God is able to do so much for us when we make ourselves vulnerable, and when we open ourselves to accepting His love and mercy. What a generous God! He truly thirsts for us!

"After this, aware that everything was now finished, in order that the scripture might be fulfilled, Jesus said, 'I thirst.'" John 19:28

"All things came to be through Him, and without Him nothing came to be. What came to be through Him was life, and this life was the light of the human race; the light shines in the darkness, and the darkness has not overcome it." John 1:3-5

CHAPTER 12

More Messages from Heaven

Introduction

Calvin (Duke) Patterson was blessed with revelations from Heaven from July 10, 2001, through June 28, 2012. He died suddenly on August 20, 2012.

There were seventy messages from Our Blessed Mother, twenty from Jesus, one each from St. Therese of Lisieux[27], the Archangel Gabriel, and the Holy Spirit. These were given for "All who will listen." These messages were deemed "Worthy of Instruction" in 2003 by a panel of Marian devotees; three priests and a layman.

There were also several private messages conveyed to Duke, to be shared with specific individuals among our family members and friends. Some of the messages were for Duke only.

One of our spiritual advisors, Father Ray Favret, suggested to us that when we share the messages, we do so one-at-a-time. So, my suggestion to you, the reader, is to read one each day, or each week. Reading them all, during one sitting, does not give the Holy Spirit the opportunity to teach you everything you could learn from the private revelation. It is also helpful to re-read them, perhaps months later. Like anything else that is complicated and layered, you may be impacted by one part of the message during your first reading, and a different part at another time in your life.

The following messages have been selected to share in this final chapter of All Who Will Listen.

Let Your Light Shine

Message from Our Blessed Mother, November 20, 2001

"My Angel,

"I send you my motherly love and blessings. It is my heart's desire to lead all of my children towards greater holiness. Live your faith! Let your light shine for all of the world to see. If you deny my Son before your fellow man, He will deny you before the Father.

"Hunger for those things which feed the spirit: prayer, Holy Mass, Holy Communion and the Holy Scriptures. Shun the evil that this world has to offer. Satan is very cunning and he will lead you astray if he can!

"Prayer is your greatest defense. Pray for the Holy Spirit to come into your heart. Pray for the love and peace that my Son so willingly offers. Surrender your will to my Son and walk in grace.

"Tell all who will listen. Thank you for responding to my call."

Satan is Furious

Message from Our Blessed Mother, January 2, 2002

"My Angel Child,

"For a season, Satan has held sway over the world with very little restraint from the Father. This period of time is rapidly coming to an end. Praise Jesus! More and more of God's children are turning their eyes towards Him. Mankind is in increasing numbers inviting my Son into their hearts. They yearn for His peace and love.

"This is not to imply that evil is ceasing. As a matter of fact, Satan is furious for he knows that his time is short. Just one man consumed with evil can do terrible harm. The change is that, more and more, mankind is not listening to Satan's lies. You will witness an unprecedented conversion to my Son. Praise Jesus!

"There are days of great darkness ahead, but at the same time, there will be great deeds of kindness and love. The Holy Spirit is moving in men's hearts like never before. You will see, my Angel, you will see! So do not be disheartened when you hear of great evil in this world, for there is a much more glorious and powerful good that will triumph. The hour of my Immaculate Heart's victory is near; even at the door.

"Rejoice and be exceedingly glad, my Angel. Tell my message to all who will listen.

"As always, you have my love and my heart. Go in peace to love and serve your Lord. Thank you for having responded to my call."

A Drop of Water in the Ocean of Eternity

Message from Our Blessed Mother on January 30, 2002

"My Angel,

"Do not be overly concerned with the things of this world. They are Satan's greatest snare, but can never provide true happiness. They are fleeting and false; like sand that slips between your fingers.

"What can this feeble life provide compared to eternity! Instead, store up your treasures in heaven. Strive constantly towards greater holiness. Pray for the Holy Spirit to transform your hearts.

"My Angel, tell my children to be kind to one another. Pray for love to conquer hate. In your every action and deed, share the love of Christ Jesus.

"Instead of storing up worldly possessions, give to those that are less fortunate, for great will be your reward in heaven.

"God yearns for all of His children to come to Him. He has blessed this world with many gifts. He has sent His Holy Spirit to provide direction through the Holy Eucharist. Jesus provides the gift of Himself to all who believe.

"Why do so many of my children refuse to accept God's gifts? Your life on this earth is like a drop of water in the ocean of eternity. My little ones, confess your sins and give your hearts and your lives to God. I long for all of my children to be with me forever. If you only knew what the Father has planned for you! What complete and total peace and joy!

"My children, take my Son's hand and let Him lead you. The Father, Jesus and I love you with a love that you cannot begin to imagine. We are standing here with open arms to receive you unto ourselves. Come to us!

"My Angel, tell this message to all who will listen. May the peace and love of Jesus be with you now and always. Praise Jesus! Thank you for having responded to my call."

Know Your Enemy

Note from Duke: "This message was given to me eight days ago and was mysteriously lost before Claire could send it out. Here it is, at 8:30 p.m. on April 21, 2002, and I'm just now writing it down. Satan has thrown up road blocks to stop this message. He surely does not want it to go out!"

Message from Our Lady given on April 13, 2002

"My Angel,

"At this time, Satan is strong. He is indeed like a raging lion, for he knows that his time is short!

"You must all stand up in righteous anger to Satan. Remember that he has no power over you. Your redemption was paid for in full by the blood of my Son. You are all children of God. God has claimed you as His own, but still, the decision is yours.

"So many of my children lay all their trials and tribulations at the feet of God and say it is God's Will. What a tragic mistake! Only goodness and grace flow from the throne of God. It is His will that all of His children should be happy. Know your enemy! Satan is behind all of your heartaches and distress. He will do everything in his power to create chaos, distress, confusion and fear in your life. Do not allow it! In a strong voice say, ***'In the name of My Lord and Savior, JESUS CHRIST, I demand that you depart, Satan!'*** He will surely flee. Satan and all of his demonic forces tremble at the mere name of Jesus!

"Be strong in your faith and be glad, my Angels. That is my heart's desire. This is a time of special graces. Lift up your hearts and your eyes to God and receive these graces. Love is being poured out unto you in abundance. You can be assured of that love. Confess your sins and give your heart to Jesus and His love and peace will be yours, my Angels.

"Tell all of my children who will listen. Thank you for responding to my call."

Study the Father's Holy Words

Our Lady's message of July 7, 2002

"My Angel,

"As always, I send you my motherly love and blessings. Praise be Jesus!

"I was so very pleased to see so many of my children gathered together to pray the holy rosary Wednesday night[10]. I was there amongst you, praying the *Our Father* and *Glory Be* with you. I pray that all of my children present felt my motherly love and peace.

"My Angel, how your love and devotion have grown over the course of the last year! Think of how our relationship has deepened. Not only have you come to regard me as your mother, but also as your best friend. As you speak to me as such, you are truly praying from the heart.

"Remember my little one, I have given you my permission to pass on my blessing to others. You may do this silently or you may simply say, ***'With love, peace and joy I give unto you the blessings of the most Blessed Holy Virgin Mary.'*** Also, do not forget to bestow unto others my Miraculous Medal[13]. I will guide you to those that are most in need. I shall use these holy objects to lead those that receive them to my Son.

"Tonight, I wish to speak to you about a matter that grieves my heart deeply. So many of my children are not studying the Holy Scriptures! My little ones, I tell you the truth, you cannot truly receive the gifts of the Holy Spirit unless you study the Father's Holy words. Therein lie wisdom, guidance, truth, example, understanding and so much more! Remember what my Son said, 'Man shall not live by bread alone but by every word that proceeds out of the mouth of God.' Your spiritual nourishment lies at your fingertips and yet you do not partake! It is my heart's desire that you should study the Holy Scriptures so that I may lead you towards greater holiness.

"My Angel, tell all who will listen. Praise be to Jesus for all who are sending my messages on to their friends; for your friends are sending messages on to their friends, who are sending the messages out to others, and so forth. I tell you the truth, many souls are being led to my Son.

"Thank you for having responded to my call. Go in peace to love and serve the Lord!"

Pray For Each Other

Our Lady's Message July 21, 2002

"My Angel,

"Please tell this message to all who will listen.

"My Dear Children,

"Those of you who have consecrated your hearts to my Son and who are living my message need to become more aware of the gift of Christian fellowship.

"The Father created each of you to be a gift to one another. You are all children of the Father and brothers and sisters through the precious blood shed by my Son. Thus, you should become and act more as a true family. Rejoice and learn from each other's strengths. Lift and comfort any of your brothers or sisters who have fallen. Take care to be respectful and loving to your elders. Provide for those who are less fortunate than you. Pray for each other.

"Prayer is the key to all of God's love, grace and mercy. Christian fellowship is very powerful in this respect. Whenever you come together as children of the light and pray from your hearts, all of the Angels in Heaven rejoice; as do I.

"Be very sure that those whose company you keep have also consecrated their hearts to my Son, for they will share the same morals, values, and priorities that you possess. If you spend too much time with those who are grasping for worldly possessions and pleasures, Satan will have an opportunity to slowly, and by subtle means, turn you away from the true faith.

"Spend as much time as possible with your brothers and sisters in prayer. Begin prayer groups on your own. Praise be to Jesus for those who do. It is my heart's desire that more of my children would do so! Come together to study and discuss the Holy Scriptures. The Holy Spirit will provide you with wondrous discernment. My little ones, remember too, my Son's promise that whenever two or more are gathered together in His name, there He will be also.

"Be kind, gentle and loving to one another, as the Father is to you. The peace and love of my precious Jesus be with you always. Go in that peace to love and serve the Lord. Praise be to Jesus!"

Pray the Holy Rosary From Your Heart

Our Lady's Message on August 7, 2002, 2:00 a.m.

"My Angel,

"As always I send you my motherly love and blessings.

"I have taught you how to pray the Holy Rosary from your heart and, praise be to Jesus, you have taught others. However, it is my heart's desire that all of my children should be told what I have taught you.

"The Holy Rosary must be prayed from the heart. Every, 'Hail Mary' that is said from the heart is a special gift to me. Do not rush by the Mysteries[15]. Take time to truly reflect and meditate on God's love and mercy on each mystery. So many of my children pray the Holy Rosary as if it were a race! This is not prayer from the heart and is just so much noise to me.

"Please, my dear children, come to the aid of your Mother. Pray with me for conversions. Pray with me for the ceasing of the horrible sin of abortion. The blood of the slain innocents cries out to the Father for justice. Pray with me for God's mercy. The prayer[3] that was given to Sister Faustina[23] should be on your lips always. Help me to spread the Gospel of my Son's love and mercy. When those around you sense your love and peace, they will ask you, 'Why are you always so at peace?' Please, my dear children, tell them! Do not be ashamed of your Lord and Savior!

"My angel, please tell all who will listen. Thank you for having responded to my call. Go in peace to love and serve the Lord. Praise be to Jesus!"

Praise the Father

Message from Our Lord, Jesus Christ, delivered on September 30, 2003, during the third Glorious Mystery, approximately 6:45 p.m. at Our Lady of the Holy Spirit Center, Norwood, Ohio.

"My Beloved Brother,

"My peace and love unto all that have gathered here tonight to pray with our Mother and to honor Me.

"As you enter this season of reflection and contemplation, consider the blessings, love and mercy that our Father has bestowed upon you. Praise the Father for the beauty that still flourishes upon the world. Praise Him for His infinite love, grace and mercy. I tell you the truth, you will spend eternity attempting to comprehend His love.

"Although this is considered a time for reaping, if you allow Me to enter into your hearts, it can be a time for glorious beginnings. Our Mother has taken you by the hand and led you to the Father. I yearn for all of My brothers and sisters to know the Father as I do.

"Listen to the words that our Mother has spoken to you. If you follow her guidance, her words will lead you to salvation.

"Our Mother has asked that you come to her aid in regard to the conversion of your brothers and sisters. Let your light shine in the darkness for all to see. Pray for one another. Love one another. Tell your brothers and sisters of My love for them and how I long for them to return to Me.

"My beloved brother, tell all who will listen. Thank you for having responded to My call. Go in peace knowing that I am with you always. All glory and praise be to the Father now and forever."

Other messages given to Calvin (Duke) Patterson can be viewed in Claire Patterson's previously published books: Through Mary's Eyes and Finding Grace Through Mary's Eyes; as well as in the blog: dukesallwhowilllisten.blogspot.org.

Index by Author

Glossary

1. Adoration, Adoration Chapel, Eucharistic Adoration or Eucharistic Exposition: This is a Catholic devotional practice in which the Blessed Sacrament, the Body of Christ, is adored by the faithful. A Perpetual Adoration Chapel is available twenty-four hours a day, seven days a week. When one prays in the chapel for an hour it is called a "holy hour." Jesus, in the form of the Host, is placed in a stand called a Monstrance.[14]

2. Apparition Hill in Medjugorje: A place where the Blessed Mother first appeared to six visionaries in 1981. Pilgrims have access to the hill, but it is not an easy climb.

3. Chaplet of the Divine Mercy, Divine Mercy Chaplet: This is the prayer given to St. Faustina by Jesus. This prayer is said on rosary beads. One prays the Divine Mercy Chaplet to ask God to "Have mercy on me and on the whole world." In the Divine Mercy image, Jesus stands with his right hand up, as in giving a blessing. His left hand holds his garment open over His heart. Red and white light rays pour from His heart symbolizing His endless stream of mercy. Beneath his feet are the words, "Jesus, I trust in You!"

4. Christ Renews His Parish: (A.K.A. CRHP, now referred to as "Welcome") This is a retreat designed to help members of a parish grow in their relationship with God. It is generally from Friday evening or Saturday morning until Sunday afternoon. It is a time to pray, and think about priorities. It is a time to get to know others in

the parish and grow as a community. It is an opportunity to examine, rediscover, and intensify one's personal relationship with Christ.

5. Cursillo: This is a movement where the lay faithful, working together with our priests and bishops, use the Cursillo method to find, form, sustain and link lay leaders for Christ and His church. Cursillo is a means of supporting Christian community.

6. Doctor of the Catholic Church: This is a title given by the Catholic Church to saints recognized as having made a significant contribution to theology or doctrine through their research, study, or writing. A Doctor of the Church has been officially recognized for having lived a very holy, humble, self-mortifying, sacrificial life, and having been a stout defender of orthodoxy.

7. Eucharistic Minister: This is usually a parishioner, selected by the Pastor, who serves, distributes, and administers the Body and Blood of Jesus Christ during the Church services and to the homebound.

8. Five First Saturdays: This is a devotion that is one of the principal points of the Fatima message. On the First Saturday, during five consecutive months, the devotion consists of: 1. going to Confession, 2. receiving the sacrament of Holy Communion, 3. saying five decades of the rosary, 4. meditating for fifteen minutes on the mysteries of the rosary. All this is offered in reparation for the sins of blasphemy and ingratitude committed against the Immaculate Heart of Mary.

9. Healthy at Home Emergency Eviction Relief Fund: These are funds appropriated from the Federal Government for Kentuckians during the COVID-19 pandemic. The money was to pay medical, utility and rent in order to prevent accumulation of debt, future evictions and homelessness.

10. July 3: This date is the anniversary of Mary's first visit with Duke on July 3, 2001. We had invited many people to celebrate the first anniversary with us on July 3, 2002. About forty people were present. Everyone received at least one miraculous medal that had been blessed by Mary during her visit with us that night.

11. Medjugorje: This is a small town in Bosnia-Herzegovina, (former Yugoslavia) where Our Blessed Mother is reported to have appeared to visionaries daily since 1981.

12. Messages Duke received, and the miracles he experienced: For more information, read Finding Grace Through Mary's Eyes. This book is available in Christian Book stores and Amazon.

13. Miraculous Medal, also known as the Medal of Our Lady of Graces: This is a devotional medal, the design of which was originated by St. Catherine Laboure following her apparitions of the Blessed Virgin Mary in Paris, France.

14. Monstrance: This is an open or transparent receptacle in which the consecrated Host is exposed for veneration.

15. Mysteries of the rosary: They are the Joyful, Luminous, Sorrowful, and Glorious Mysteries. Each Mystery contains five focus points for meditation on Jesus' life.

16. OCIA (formerly RCIA) (Order of Christian Initiation for Adults): This is the on-going process of learning and growing in the faith, and preparing candidates for sacraments to fully enter into the Catholic faith.

17. Our Lady of Guadalupe: This is a title of Mary, the mother of Jesus, associated with a series of five Marian apparitions to a Mexican peasant, Juan Diego, in December 1531, outside present-day Mexico City.

18. Our Lady of the Holy Spirit Center: It is a former Seminary, turned Retreat Center, in Norwood, Ohio. The center exists to lead people closer to God through promoting deeper prayer and reflections, faith-filled education and the sacraments of the Catholic Church.

19. Our Lady of Light: This refers to the many presumed appearances of Our Lady of Light at Our Lady of the Holy Spirit Center in Norwood, Ohio and St. Joseph's Church in Cold Spring, Kentucky. They have not been officially approved by the Catholic Church. The thousands who witnessed the phenomena, and those who still feel Her presence and grace at The Holy Spirit Center and Our Lady's Farm, will attest to the powerful effect Our Lady of Light has had, and continues to have, in their lives.

20. Our Lady's Farm: This is a site of reported apparitions and healings in Falmouth, Kentucky. It is affiliated with Our Lady of the Holy Spirit Center.

21. Plenary (meaning "full") Indulgence: This is a special type of indulgence that, if all the requirements are met, removes all temporal punishment due to one's sin.

22. Scapular (Latin for shoulders): This is something usually worn under clothing. It is generally a circular, thirty-inch piece of yarn or ribbon, with two small brown or green squares of cloth on either end. One rests on the back and one on the front of the person wearing it. It is blessed. It is a reminder to emulate Jesus at all times.

23. St. Faustina, Sister Faustina: On February 22, 1931, Sister Faustina was visited by Jesus, who presented himself as the "King of Divine Mercy."[3]

24. St. Maria Goretti: Young Maria was eleven years old when she became a victim of attempted rape and subsequent murder. While dying from multiple stab wounds, she forgave the man who attacked and murdered her.

25. St. Padre Pio: Pio of Pietrelcina (born Francesco Forgione; 1887 –1968), generally known as Padre Pio, was an Italian Capuchin friar, priest, stigmatist and mystic.

26. (Pope) St. John Paul II: born Karl Wojityla in 1920. He served as Pope from 1978 until his death in 2005. He was canonized in 2014.

27. St. Therese, the Little Flower of Lisieux: She died at the age of twenty-four from tuberculosis after living an obscure life, including nine years as a Carmelite nun. Pope Pius X called her "the greatest saint of modern times." She is the patron saint of priests and missionaries. October 1 is her feast day.

28. St. Vincent de Paul Society: This is an international Catholic organization of volunteers who provide services to the poor, with needs such as medicine, transportation, rent and utilities.

29. "Walking With Purpose": This is a bible study program for women.

30. Works of Mercy: The Corporal Works of Mercy are: to feed the hungry, to give drink to the thirsty, to clothe the naked, to shelter the homeless, to visit the sick, to ransom the captive, to bury the dead. The Spiritual Works of Mercy are: to instruct the ignorant, to counsel the doubtful, to admonish sinners, to bear wrongs patiently, to forgive offenses willingly, to comfort the afflicted, to pray for the living and the dead.

"Finally, brothers, whatever is true, whatever is honorable, whatever is just, whatever is pure, whatever is lovely, whatever is gracious, if there is any excellence and if there is anything worthy of praise, think about these things." Philippians 4:8